CW00537764

OSPREY MILITARY CAMPAIGN SERIES: 46

LAKE PEIPUS 1242
BATTLE OF THE ICE

SERIES EDITOR: LEE JOHNSON

OSPREY MILITARY CAMPAIGN SERIES: 46

LAKE PEIPUS 1242

BATTLE OF THE ICE

DAVID NICOLLE

OSPREY
MILITARY

First published in Great Britain in 1996 by Osprey, a division of Reed Books Limited, Michelin House, 81 Fulham Road, London SW3 6RB and Auckland, Melbourne, Singapore and Toronto

© Copyright 1996 Reed International Books Ltd.

All rights reserved. Apart from any fair dealing for the purpose of private study, research, criticism or review, as permitted under the Copyright, Designs and Patents Act, 1988, no part of this publication may be reproduced, stored in a retrieval system, or transmitted in any form or by any means electronic, electrical, chemical, mechanical, optical, photocopying, recording or otherwise, without the prior written permission of the copyright owner. Enquiries should be addressed to the Publishers.

ISBN 1 85532 553 5

Military Editor: Iain MacGregor
Designed by TT Designs

Colour bird's-eye-view illustrations by Peter Harper.
Cartography by Micromap.
Wargaming Lake Peipus by Jim Webster.

Filmset in Singapore.
Printed through World Print Ltd., Hong Kong

*For a catalogue of all books published by Osprey Military
please write to:*

Osprey, 2nd Floor, Unit 6, Spring Gardens, Tinworth Street, Vauxhall, London SE11 5EH

Key to military series symbols

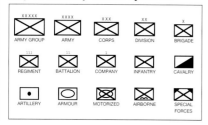

Dedication

For Luda, the two Sashas and Tolya.

PAGE 2 **A late 12th century tapestry from Hedmark. (Museum of Applied Arts, Oslo, Norway)**

PAGE 3 **German bronze aquamanile in the form of a fully armoured knight wearing a great helm. This sort of metal work was exported all over Europe. (inv. nr. 9094, National Museum, Copenhagen, Denmark)**

CONTENTS

EASTERN EUROPE – c.1223–1242

N

| 0 | 100 | 200 Miles |
| 0 | 100 | 200 | 300 Km |

Kingdom of Denmark
Baltic Crusader States
Russian States
Mongol Empire
Mongol Campaigns: 1223–1242
Northern Crusade Campaigns: 1199–1240
Frontiers
Undefined frontiers

Lapps

Ugrians

Finns

NORWAY

Swedes

Abo

Helsinki

Beloozero

Vologda

Ustyug

SWEDEN

Oslo

Stockholm

Danes

Tallinn

Novgorod

Rostov

Suzdal

Vladimir

Bulgar

Pskov

Murom

Riga

Moscow

DENMARK

Lund

Polotsk

Tula

Ryazan

Roskilde

Lithuanians

Vitebsk

Smolensk

Vilna

MONGOL
EMPIRE

Stettin

Prussians

Minsk

Marienwerder

Poznan

POLISH
STATES

Turov

Novgorod
Severskii

Prague

Vladimir
Volhynskii

Chernigov

Kiev

Pereyaslavl

GERMAN
EMPIRE

Cracow

Galich

Vienna

Buda

HUNGARY

Venice

Cherson

Venetian

GEORGIA

BLACK SEA

SERBIA

Sofia

BULGARIA

Trabzon

Byzantine

GEORGIA

Byzantine

Constantinople

Seljuks

Naples

LATIN
EMPIRE

Thessaloniki

Byzantine

Ayyubids

ORIGINS OF THE CAMPAIGN

THE EASTERN BALTIC

By the late 12th century the eastern Baltic, from Prussia to Finland, was the last major bastion of European paganism. This was seen as an affront by the Church, but the Balts and Finns of the area were not barbarians. Their homeland's winters were cold, though not as ferocious as those of neighbouring Russia. Nevertheless, it was a region of forests, lakes, marshes and rivers, with little room for agriculture.

A borderline between northern coniferous and southern deciduous forests ran through what is now Estonia, where the silver birch featured most prominently in folklore. In the east a bleak region of swamp and marsh with thousands of tiny streams and several great rivers, all of which froze in winter, separated the Baltic peoples from Russia.

The indigenous people spoke Baltic languages in the south, Finnish tongues in the north. In the west the prosperous Prussians were conquered by German Crusaders in the 13th century, and their language died out in the 17th century. Some of the fiercer Lithuanians in the east remained pagan until 1386; they not only retained their independence but by the 15th century they had carved out their own vast empire from the Baltic to the Black Sea.

To the north were the Livs and Letts of what is now Latvia, and the Est of Estonia. An early 20th century historian wrote of the latter: *"At a much lower level than the Prussians stood the Letts and the sombre Finnish Estonians who formed nothing better than petty states with very little community life, dwelling in the monotonous wastes of their prairies, bogs and pine-forests, unacquainted with the luxuries of oaks or the liveliness of royal deer-hunts."*

Nevertheless, the Estonians, who spoke a Finnish rather than Baltic dialect, were the most likely of all to rebel against Crusader domination. Across the Gulf of Finland were the largely agricultural Suomi and, further inland, the Tavastian or Emi hunting tribes of Finland. Finally there were the nomadic Saami or Lapps, who ranged the Arctic coast from the White sea to central Norway.

The paganism of these northern peoples was a sophisticated form of shamanism and, not surprisingly, a source of fear to medieval Christendom. In the 11th century Adam of Bremen wrote of the eastern Baltic: *"Its people, too, are utterly ignorant of the God of the Christians. They worship serpents and birds and also sacrifice to them live men whom they buy from merchants. The men are carefully inspected all over to see that they are without bodily defect on account of which, they say, the serpents would reject them."*

The anonymous author of the *Livonian Rhymed Chronicle* knew better, but still found Baltic paganism daunting: *"The Estonians,"* he wrote, *"are pagans also, and there are many mothers sons of them. That is because their land is so broad and so spread out that I cannot describe it. They have so many*

Estonian dagger-blades, decorated leather sheaths and iron axes of the 10th-12th centuries. (Museum of Estonian History, Tallinn, Estonia)

powerful men and so many provinces full of them that I do not want to talk more about them."

Sadly, the mysteries of ancient Baltic paganism would later appeal to the paganism of 20th century Nazis; as one German historian wrote: *"A semi-secret priesthood, whose members were rarely seen by their co-nationals and never by strangers, fostered consecrated serpents in shrines made of oak-branches, while keeping alight on stone altars the odoriferous amber-fires kindled in honour of the gods of a faith that bore few traces of the usual characteristics of primitive religions."*

In fact, by the 14th century the Lithuanians could be described as 'pagans against their will', their religion having become a cultural defence against aggressive Christian neighbours. By the 12th century, however, many Letts and Estonians had been peacefully converted by the

Estonian spearhead, ceremonially 'sacrificed' sword, stirrups and bridle of the 10th-12th centuries. (Museum of Estonian History, Tallinn, Estonia)

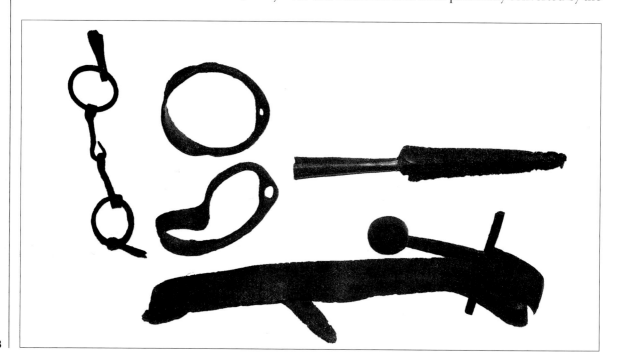

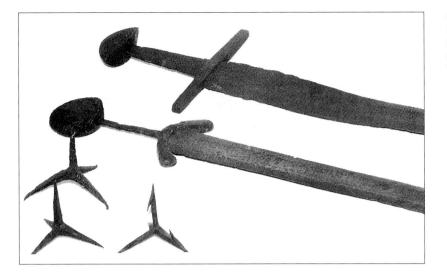

German swords and calthrops used by Estonian tribal warriors in the 13th-14th centuries. (Museum of Estonian History, Tallinn, Estonia)

Russian Orthodox Church, and the Estonian provinces along the western side of Lake Peipus were probably largely Orthodox by 1095.

The Finnish-speaking peoples, including the Est, had a looser social organisation than the Balts, but everywhere the basic unit was the extended family. These families formed part of larger clans which could themselves join to form tribes in time of war. The foremost male of each family was its senior or 'elder', who would join other elders in a clan or tribal council. Sometimes a successful elder would be recognised as a chief or war-leader, though this was rare. Powerful families provided a warrior class, often of horsemen, who lived by farming and cattle raising, while at the bottom of the social scale were slaves captured in war.

Military pressure from the northern Crusades led to a distinct militarisation of Baltic society during the 12th and 13th centuries. Though there were no indigenous states, there were fortifications and little towns. In Estonia each *kihelkond*, or district, had one or two earth and timber forts which, governed by elders, served as places of refuge for surrounding villages. Like the fortifications of neighbouring Slav lands, their internal buildings clustered against the outer wall, leaving a central area open, save for a well. By the early 13th century several of these fortresses had already formed the nuclei of towns, which had grown up as a result of trade with the outside world. Estonia and Finland, for example, had been under strong Scandinavian influence since the early Middle Ages but, like Latvia, Lithuania and Prussia to the south, Estonia was also in trading contract with Byzantium, the Muslim world and Central Asia via Russia. While contact with Scandinavia was by sea, contact with Russia was by river.

The degree of early medieval Russian control over what are now the Baltic States is obscured by nationalistic passions. Vladimir the Great, the first Christian ruler of Russia, may have briefly dominated much of the area at the start of the 11th century, while the east Estonian town of Tartu (known as Dorpat in German and Yurev in Russian) was founded by Yaroslav the Wise of Russian Novgorod in 1030.

The eastern Baltic was not a particularly peaceful area, even before the Crusaders arrived. Stronger tribes raided the weaker for slaves, while the most powerful even plundered their Scandinavian and Russian

Saint Peter wielding a heavy mid 13th century German sword of war in a carving of the arrest of Jesus. (*in situ* Cathedral, Naumberg, Germany)

neighbours. Warfare normally consisted of sudden raids in over-whelming force, followed by a swift retreat before the defenders could rally. Raids aimed at procuring prisoners, booty and prestige, rather than the conquest of land or imposition of tribute. Women and children were the favoured captives; men were often slaughtered since it was too easy for them to escape. Surplus slaves were sold to merchants, for resale in Byzantium. This style of warfare gave the Baltic and Finnish peoples the military skills that would be used against, and in alliance with, both Crusaders and Russians.

THE NORTHERN CRUSADES

The Catholic military offensive in the Baltic never enjoyed the prestige of the Middle Eastern Crusades but it had far greater results: the great majority of Baltic peoples remain members of western (Catholic or Protestant) churches to this day. German and Scandinavian merchants appear to have undertaken the first military offensives to consolidate their markets. Next came the Church and the Military Order of Sword Brethren, followed by Crusaders from the German, Danish and Swedish nobility, eager to carve out new estates. Only later did the Teutonic Knights appear on the scene, after their predecessors had quarrelled among themselves.

The men involved in these northern Crusades came from countries which were themselves changing fast. In Germany, for example, the late

12th and 13th centuries saw a steep decline in the authority of the emperor and near anarchy as a result of his power struggle with the Pope. Denmark and Sweden were also becoming more obviously 'European' as they loosened their links with Russia, Byzantium and the Muslim world.

Officially the Baltic Crusade began as a small-scale affair while the Fourth Crusade was being prepared. At first Pope Innocent III merely called upon northern Germans to defend the new and vulnerable Church in Livonia. Even when the Northern Crusade went onto the offensive, it was aimed at pagan Balts and Finns rather than Orthodox Christian Russians. Meanwhile the papacy ensured that it remained secondary to the main Mediterranean thrust against Islam. Danes had been raiding the eastern Baltic coast since 1191, but in the early 13th century, under Waldemar the Great, this developed into a determined effort to create a Danish empire around the entire Baltic, including northern Germany. In 1219 Bishop Albert Von Buxhoeved of Riga, alarmed by a revival of Russian interest in his area, promised Waldemar that he could keep any pagan lands he conquered. A year later the Danes built a fortress on the rock of Tallinn, now the capital of Estonia. Unfortunately the Sword Brethren were also planning to take Estonia, so the seeds of conflict were sewn. Although the dream of a Danish Baltic empire soon collapsed, with Danish domination of northern Germany crushed at the battle of Bornhöved in 1227, Denmark retained northern Estonia until 1346. Nevertheless, the future lay with the Crusading Military Orders: first the Sword Brethren and later the Teutonic Knights.

Danish efforts to dominate the Baltic frightened the German colonists in Livonia into strengthening their own position by conquering their pagan neighbours. Bishop Albert Von Buxhoeved also won recognition from the German emperor as a 'territorial prince' – like so many other bishops in Germany. Meanwhile he and the Bishop of Estonia

A side-view of late 13th century carved capital showing Teutonic Knights jousting. (inv. MZM/ DA/ 5, Malbork Castle Museum, Poland)

founded the Sword Brethren to extend and defend Christian Livonia. Bishop Albert would, however, soon quarrel with his own creation, as the Sword Brethren wanted to conquer Estonian tribes in an area either promised to the Danes or already tributary to the Russian city of Pskov, where Albert's brother, Theodoric Von Buxhoeved was marrying into the ruling family.

The fierce Est tribes of Ungannia on the western side of Lake Peipus, with their powerful fortress at Tartu, remained a barrier to Crusader expansion. Tartu was under an elder named Vetseke, but also had a Russian garrison, since it owed tenuous allegiance to Pskov. Nevertheless, the Sword Brethren pressed ahead and, being unable to stop them, Bishop Albert encouraged his brother, Bishop Hermann Von Buxhoeved, to join in. Hermann and the Sword Brethren even drew lots to

Embossed copper altar-front showing the Massacre of the Innocents, Swedish, late 12th-early 13th century. The soldier is wearing a form of lamellar armour. (From Broddetorp, Västergötland, inv. nr. 4674, Statens Historiska Museum, Stockholm, Sweden. Photograph Söven Hall)

Moravian manuscript illustration of a battle between Israelites and Philistines, 1212-1220. The fact that some soldiers on both sides are wearing scale or lamellar armour suggests that such eastern styles of protection were used in 13th century central as well as eastern Europe. (Hours of the Virgin, M.739, f. f.17v, Pierpont Morgan Lib., New York, USA)

decide who would have this unconquered territory: Hermann drew Ungannia itself, while the Sword Brethren drew Saccalia to the west. In 1224, after a bitter siege, the Crusaders took Tartu, massacring the entire garrison except one man, who was only left to carry the news back to Russia.

Bishop Hermann of Tartu now set out to make himself as powerful a prince as was his brother Bishop Albert of Riga. He gave fiefs to his numerous relatives, encouraged other Germans to settle as a new feudal aristocracy and brought priests to convert the local Estonians. The following year Hermann Von Buxhoeved was recognised as a prince-bishop, giving him greater authority when dealing with Danes and Sword Brethren.

The papacy now took a closer interest in these northern Crusades, to prevent independent monarchies emerging as they had in the Crusader Middle East. The local population was also converted, sometimes at the point of a sword, in a manner not seen again until the conquest of the New World in the 16th century.

The Order of the Hospital of St. Mary of the Germans of Jerusalem, or the Teutonic Knights, as they are better known, originated at the Crusader siege of Acre in 1189/90 but was reconstructed as a Military Order, based upon that of the Templars, in 1198. Early in the 13th century the Teutonic Knights helped defend the eastern frontier of Hungary but they were thrown out after attempting to carve out their own autonomous state. The idea of creating a state may have been deeply embedded in the Teutonic Order from the start, and Grand Master Hermann Von Salza certainly demanded freedom of action before agreeing to fight the Prussians in 1226.

Though Prussia was intended as a training ground for the Middle East, it was here that the Teutonic Knights had their greatest impact on European history, carving out their own independent state. Nevertheless, the Order did have to share authority with the local bishops, and they sometimes quarrelled with the powerful merchants of Riga. Like the Sword Brethren and the German settlers, they tended to regard the natives as inferiors who had been 'slaves of the Devil' and were now 'slaves of Christ'. As an old Estonian poem put it:

Puff yourselves up, you Germans
Thinking yourself better than anyone in the world
You dislike all that we poor Estonians do
May you be placed, therefore, into the depths of Hell.

The Crusader conquest of the Esti citadel of Muhu in 1227, painted by G. Kangilaski in 1961. This illustration was based on the latest archaeological evidence for the construction of the wooden fortress and for Crusader assault techniques. (Museum of Estonian History, Tallinn, Estonia)

In later centuries the militaristic character of the Military Order's state led some German historians to glorify it as the foundation for Hohenzollern imperial rule in 19th century Germany. Just before the Second World War a Nazi historian took these unpleasant parallels still further: "*This was the hour of the birth of a new Germany. The Teutonic Order, engaged in establishing in the Prussian country an independent State, became the interpreter of the national will, expressed in a powerful longing for more eastern territory, and gave this struggle against the heathen a direction corresponding to national interests.*"

While the Teutonic Knights were opening a second front against the pagans in Prussia, in Livonia tensions were rising between Danes, Sword Brethren and Bishop Hermann of Tartu. In 1234 the papal legate William of Modena arrived to sort things out. Hermann was now restricted to Tartu, losing his other bishopric, of Leal, though he and the Von Buxhoeved family remained very powerful.

Two years later a large army of visiting 'seasonal' Crusaders and a substantial proportion of the Sword Brethren's elite knights were crushed at the battle of the Saule river. The Master of the Sword Brethren was killed and the power of the Order was so broken that its remnants had to be absorbed by the Teutonic Knights to ensure the survival of the Crusader state in Livonia. But this again led to tensions with Waldemar of Denmark, who had himself hoped to take over the Brethren's land. In 1238 the Pope, who alone had authority to disband the Sword Brethren, gave Estonia to the Danes and Latvia to the Teutonic Knights. The Pope may already have been planning to use the Teutonic Knights against Orthodox Russia.

The Knights were now seriously overstretched, contributing to the defence of a huge frontier from Poland to Lake Peipus. Their command structure was also influenced by the Order's sudden change of fortune. While the Grand Master was primarily concerned with the Holy Land, a promising young officer named Dietrich Von Grüningen had been second in command to Hermann Balke, Master of the Knights in the Baltic. Balke retired in 1238 and, according to some sources, Von Grüningen took over but only in Livonia, not Prussia.

Dietrich Von Grüningen was himself often called away, leaving the Teutonic Knights of Livonia under the authority of Andreas Von Felben from 1241 to 1242. But other sources suggest that Von Grüningen was passed over in favour of Von Felben in 1240, only becoming local Master of the Teutonic Knights in 1242 or 1244 – after the battle of Lake Peipus.

Tensions between the Catholic and Greek or Orthodox Churches had been rising since the 11th century. The Roman papacy hoped to take over the Orthodox east, and in 1204 the Fourth Crusade captured the Byzantine capital of Constantinople. For a while it seemed that Latin

RIGHT **The citadel or fortified old town of Novgorod from the air, photographed before the destruction wrought by the Nazis during the Second World War. The 12th century Cathedral of Santa Sophia stands within the 15th century walls and towers which, in turn, followed the line of earlier medieval wooden fortifications. The river Volkhov is on the left.**

The oldest part of the Toompea Castle in Tallinn was built by the Sword Brethren in 1227-1229, though like the rest of the castle it was rebuilt in the 15th century. (Author's photograph)

domination could be achieved through force of arms and, after the capture of Tartu in Estonia, several unsuccessful efforts were made to persuade the Russian state of Novgorod to accept the Catholic rite. But at the same time Europe's enthusiasm for crusading was in decline, particularly in Germany. Ambition, in fact, was outstripping ability.

Novgorod between the Nemtsy and the Mongols

A medieval Russian proverb used to say: *"Who can stand against God and the Great Novgorod?"* Novgorod the Great, dominating northern Russia, was indeed a powerful city. Russia itself was a vast but thinly populated land divided into ten principalities named after their main cities. Each was supposedly ruled by a descendant of Rurik, founder of the medieval Russian state. Though now in decline, Kiev was still the leading principality and throne of the *Veliki Knez*, or Grand Prince. Meanwhile the lesser *knezes* (princes) had also been losing power to the *boyars*, or aristocracy and urban merchant class.

Novgorod itself lay near the edge of the coniferous forest zone and was virtually surrounded by swamps which offered little scope for agriculture. It existed solely for trade, and here its dismal location on the Volkhov river was an advantage, since this led via Lake Ladoga and the Neva river to the Gulf of Finland and, via several overland portages, down the Dvina to the Baltic, the Dnepr to Kiev and Byzantium and the Volga to Central Asia. The city of Novgorod was said to have been founded by Slovene, rather than Russian, tribesmen, who had migrated north in the 6th century. In the late 9th century Kiev sent a Varangian (Russo-Norse) garrison to Novgorod and in 968 the city asked the ruler of Kiev to appoint his son Vladimir as their own first *knez*; Vladimir's uncle became Novgorod's first *posadnik*, or mayor. The pattern was thus

Carved stone icon of Saint George made in 1234. In this example of Russian religious art, the scale cuirass, shield and spear may reflect some of the military equipment used in central Russia. (*in situ* Cathedral of Saint George, Yureve-Polskom, Russia)

A model of the wood-paved streets, wooden houses and other buildings of medieval Novgorod, based upon extensive excavations carried out by Russian archaeologists since the Second World War. (Kremlin Museum, Novgorod, Russia)

set for Novgorod's commercial power as well as its tense relations with the ruling princes of medieval Russia.

Novgorod's special character was reflected in its layout: it had a large community of foreign merchants living on the east bank of the Volkhov, facing the fortified Santa Sofia area on the west bank. Here the city's three quarrelsome quarters may originally have been inhabited by the three peoples who founded Novgorod – Slavs, Finns and Balts. All were now Russians, since those who became Orthodox Christians were accepted as 'Rus'.

By the late 12th century the Bishop of Novgorod was nominal head of the city and its huge trading empire. Only occasionally could a *knez* be imposed from outside: most had to be invited in by the *veche*, or town council. In turn, the frequency with which *knezes* were evicted reflected competing factions among the *boyars* and merchants who really dominated Novgorod. But despite its wealth and its militia, the city could seldom defend itself from a serious outside threat. On such occasions a *knez* was invited to lead Novgorod's own forces and to strengthen them with his own *druzhina*, or private army.

Novgorod was the first Russian state to push eastward, and by 1100 its merchants had even crossed the northern Ural mountains into the endless swamps of the Ob basin. Novgorod's direct rule soon reached the Arctic, what was called the 'Land of Midnight'. Scattered *pogost* (administrative centres) controlled the Finnish and Ugrian natives, collecting tribute and keeping open the river routes. Though cold and desolate, these northern wastes produced a wealth of furs, walrus ivory and dried fish. The furs gave Novgorod the money to buy the food its own bleak forests could not supply. Sometimes Novgorod's merchants were tempted to become *ushkúynik*, or river pirates, while the poorer classes also regarded the north as a land of opportunity – a medieval version of America's Wild West, to be settled by peasant communes, aristocratic *boyar* estates and Russian Orthodox monasteries.

Campaigns further east proved costly. One army sent against the Ugrians in 1079 simply disappeared without trace, and in 1193 a force sent to the Pechora river was virtually wiped out. The Russians even came to believe that an evil people had been locked behind the Ural mountains, when Alexander the Great asked God to free the world from such terrible folk. The only entrance was believed to be a tiny copper gate in a ring of rock which would be opened on Judgement Day. Ugrians who lived west of the Urals promoted this myth, presumably so that they could control the region's fur trade.

Closer to home Novgorod also dominated its so-called 'younger brother', the city of Pskov. This was a turbulent autonomous *prisgorod,* or subordinate city, under a *posadnik* sent from Novgorod. Pskov was set amid fertile agricultural land – a luxury Novgorod lacked.

Donor figures on an icon of saints Alexai and Petrov from Novgorod, 1294. The bearded figure is dressed as a Russian nobleman or prince, the other as a warrior. (Kremlin Museum, Novgorod, Russia)

Novgorod's relations with the other states were also changing. The great city of Kiev had declined since its sacking by Vladimir-Suzdal – an event sometimes called the victory of 'forest Russia' over 'steppe Russia' – and central Russia had become the powerbase of the Grand Prince. Nevertheless, the Russian city-states remained linked by religion, culture and, to a great extent, language, while a general sense that the Russian Orthodox Christian world was not part of Latin Catholic western Europe grew ever stronger.

Before the coming of the Crusaders, Russian Novgorod, Polotsk and Volhynia showed little interest in their shared frontier with the Baltic peoples. As long as the river routes remained open the Russians seemed content. Even though little effort was made to convert the indigenous peoples, Orthodox Christianity had been spreading among the tribes on both sides of the Gulf of Finland, and this was soon to lead to a clash with Swedish Crusaders spreading Catholic Christianity from the west. By 1200 Novgorod had also imposed its suzerainty over the Finnish Karelians, Izhora and Vod, partly to stop them raiding Novgorodian territory but partly to forestall a Swedish takeover.

As Novgorod erected this buffer zone of vassal tribes in the north, Russian hegemony over the pagan tribes of the lower Dvina river had crumbled away. Efforts by Pskov and Novgorod to help the Estonians resist Crusader attack between 1211 and 1218 also achieved little. In reality the Russian *knezes* were preoccupied with internal squabbles, while Novgorod made up for the loss of western tribute through greatly increased trade with German and Scandinavian newcomers. Then, in 1223, came the first devastating Mongol invasion of southern Russia, in a year which also saw an outbreak of plague in the Baltic area, an Estonian rising against the Crusaders and the short-lived installation of a combined Pskov–Novgorod garrison in Tartu. While the Swedes and Danes were seen as potential problems, the unification of the Military Orders of Sword Brethren and Teutonic Knights was regarded as favourable. As the *Chronicle of Novgorod* stated: *"In this year (1237) the Nemtsii came in great strength from beyond the sea to Riga and all united there; both the men of Riga and all the Chud land (Estonia), and the men of Pskov also sent a help of two hundred men. And they went against the godless Lithuanians, and thus for our sins they were defeated by the godless pagans, and only one man in ten came back to his home."*

The rising power of the Lithuanians was, in fact, a greater menace than the Crusaders, though this threat really began when Mindaugas united the tribes under his rule in 1238.

Within Novgorod and Pskov there was a clear division of opinion about how to deal with the Crusaders, especially in the light of the looming Mongol threat. Some Russians wanted to come to terms with these newcomers, while others favoured resistance under a *knez* nominated by the Grand Prince of Russia. Meanwhile there was already intermarriage between leading families from the expanding Crusader enclaves and those of north-western Russia, in particular with the Mstislavich princely dynasty of Smolensk, who were also occasional rulers of Novgorod. Pskov, however, overthrew Vladimir Mstislavich, brother of bishops Albert and Hermann, but the Sword Brethren became a threat after they and Bishop Hermann conquered Tartu in what Pskov regarded as its own territory. Since neither Pskov nor Novgorod could fight the Crusaders alone, those who favoured resistance looked to the Vsevolodovich princely dynasty, rivals of the Mstislavich family, for their salvation. As a result, Yaroslav Vsevolodovich was at various times *knez* of

An early medieval church and a later monastery inside the fortifications of Pskov. Russian Orthodox monasteries were normally fortified and even had their own armed guards.

Novgorod as well as *Veliki Knez* of both Kiev and Vladimir.

In 1228, following unseasonal rains which ruined the harvest, the still semi-pagan poor of Novgorod rioted. This led the *veche* to replace the city's pro-Vsevolodovich militia commander with Boris Negochevich, a member of the rival party. Rather than agree to this move, Varoslav Vsevolodovich ordered his sons and representatives, Fedor and Alexandre, to leave the city. Thereupon the *veche* asked the ruler of the powerful southern city of Chernigov to be their *knez* – further confusing an already complex power struggle. A few years later Pskov wanted Yaroslav Vsevolodovich's eldest son, Fedor, as their *knez*, but Fedor died and Yaroslav sent his brother-in-law Gyurgi instead. That same year the struggle between the Mstislavich and Vsevolodovich families for control of Novgorod ended with victory for the latter, and Yaroslav Vsevolodovich sent his second son, Alexandre – the future Alexandre Nevskii, to be the city's *knez*.

While all this was going on, the Mongols had been preparing a second and permanent invasion. Russia had long experience of raids by peoples from the steppes, and had itself been equally willing to invade the steppes when the balance of power was in its favour. Nevertheless, a symbiotic relationship based on alliances, intermarriage and trade meant that peace between Russians and Turkish steppe nomads had been the norm (the 'nomad plague' was, in fact, a myth). However, the Mongols were different. By the time of their second invasion in 1237–40, they had been so influenced by Chinese civilisation that the Mongol ruling elite were no longer nomads. Part of the Mongol army was probably Christian, of the eastern Nestorian sect. Certainly their military technology betrayed enormous Chinese influence, while the effectiveness of Mongol armies was based on a new, rigid discipline which replaced the loose kinship ties seen in previous Turkish steppe cultures.

The Mongol penetration of northern Russia in the winter of 1237/38 came as a great shock to Novgorod, since earlier steppe raiders never reached that far. Alexandre had prepared no defences and instead Novgorod fell back on its traditional policy of bowing to the inevitable, particularly if that did not interfere with trade. The people also prayed for divine help, and this seemed to have worked when the invading Mongols turned back only a few miles from the city. What had actually saved Novgorod was a sudden spring thaw which had left the invaders floundering in deep Russian mud. Nevertheless, Alexandre stuck with a policy of loyal submission rather than suicidal resistance, and where Novgorod led, other Russian cities eventually followed. Economic and cultural life survived and in some ways flourished under Mongol rule, while the tendency for Orthodox Russia to separate itself from Catholic western Europe was reinforced.

Carved stone icon of Saint Demetrius, from south-western Russia, 1200-1250. The style of armour is almost entirely Byzantine, but the sword could have come straight from Central Asian art of a few centuries earlier, perhaps reflecting the influence of nomadic peoples such as the Kipchaqs in this part of Russia. (Historical Museum, Kamenez-Podolsk, Ukraine)

THE OPPOSING COMMANDERS

CRUSADER LEADERS

Several important figures were involved in the campaigns of 1240–1242, yet the sources are unclear about who commanded the Crusader army at Lake Peipus. Bishop Hermann Von Buxhoeved of Tartu was almost certainly there, but others who might have been expected to take part did not, probably because they disapproved of the entire Crusade against Novgorod.

The Von Buxhoeved family were prime movers in much of the conquest of Livonia and Estonia, virtually forming an ecclesiastical dynasty in this region. Hermann himself was a nephew of Hartwig, the powerful prince-archbishop of Hamburg and Bremen in north Germany, but as the youngest of five brothers, he was not the leading member of his generation. That honour went to Albert Von Buxhoeved, Bishop of Riga, while Theodoric married a daughter of Vladimir Mstislavich of Pskov, Engelbert became a prior at Riga and Rothmar a prior at Tartu (before dying in 1234). All died before the Novgorod Crusade.

Hermann Von Buxhoeved had been an abbot in Bremen when the Archbishop of Magdeburg made him Bishop of Estonia, in 1220. Thereafter he soon got involved in the quarrel between his brother Bishop Albert of Riga, the Danes and the Order of Sword Brethren. Hermann even managed to insult King Waldemar of Denmark, which suggests that his character was similar to his brutal brother Albert. More is known about Albert, who was described as *"one of the greatest churchmen, diplomats and empire-builders of the early thirteenth century. Able, ambitious, and greedy . . . Albert came to Livonia rather as a prince than as a preacher"*. According to the *Livonian Rhymed Chronicle* Hermann was *"no less venerable"* than Albert, and he certainly made a comparable impact on eastern Estonia before his death in 1248.

The most important military leader in Crusader Livonia during the Crusade against Novgorod was Andreas Von Felben, Landmeister or provincial commander of the Teutonic Knights in Riga. Despite being an ex-member of the Sword Brethren, Andreas seems to have disapproved of the campaign: although he took part in the conquest of Pskov, he stayed out of subsequent operations and was not present at the battle of Lake Peipus.

Andreas Von Felben's family came from Utrecht in the Netherlands, so Andreas could have been related to Arnestus de Vulven, the Teutonic

Incised tomb-slab from Holme castle, early 13th century. Though crude in style, this is a rare example of an illustration of a knight of the northern Crusades from Livonia. (National Museum, Riga, Latvia)

Knights' marshal in Acre, or he could have come from a village in Austria. Despite his 'arm's length' approach to the Novgorod Crusade, Andreas felt obliged to retire briefly to Holland after the disastrous battle of Lake Peipus. Nevertheless, he was back in Livonia by 1243, serving as Vice Landmeister under Dietrich Von Grüningen.

RUSSIAN LEADERS

As ruler of Novgorod and eventually Grand Prince of Russia, far more is known about Alexandre Nevskii than about his Crusader opponents. Yet this abundance of information can obscure the real man because so much is either medieval hero worship or a modern attempt to use Alexandre for political reasons. His biography, entitled *The Story about the Feats and Life of Grand Prince Alexandre Nevskii*, was a *skazanie* or 'epic' surviving in a 15th century manuscript from Pskov. Nevertheless, its author claimed to have met Alexandre and to have stuck very closely to events. The description in the *Chronicle of Novgorod* is more obviously hero worship: "*In truth his rule would not endure unless God willed it. His stature exceeds that of other men, his voice is like a trumpet among men, his face is a face like Joseph's, whom the Egyptian pharaoh made a second pharaoh in Egypt. His strength is like the strength of Samson the Strong, and God has given him the wisdom of Solomon, and the courage of the Roman Caesar Vespasian, who took captive the entire land of Judea.*"

Alexandre's collaboration with the Mongol conquerors has, however, been an embarrassment to Russian historians ever since. Some pre-Soviet historians claimed that Alexandre "*saved the soul of Orthodox Russia*" by defeating the invading Catholic Crusaders before submitting to Mongol overlordship. Soviet historians indulged in verbal gymnastics to deal with Alexandre and the Mongols, while some modern Western historians simply seem keen to debunk the Alexandre myth.

The facts indicate a capable and ruthless military commander but, above all, a skilful and far-sighted politician. His background was typical of the almost nomadic ruling class of medieval Russia. His family took its name from Alexandre's great-great-great-grandfather, Vseolod Yaroslavich one of the heroes of 11th century Russia.

Born around 1220, Alexandre spent most of his youth in the principality of Pereyaslavl in southern Russia, which was ruled by his father, though he also lived for several years in Novgorod in the far north. Alexandre came from a family of eight warlike brothers, an unknown number of sisters and five male cousins, most of whom became rulers of one or more Russian states. When his elder brother Fedor died, Alexandre became the senior brother, and in 1236 he was left by his father as sole *knez* of Novgorod. In 1239 Alexandre married a daughter of the ruler of the

German bronze aquamanile in the form of a fully armoured knight wearing a great helm. This sort of metalwork was exported all over Europe. (inv. nr. 9094, National Museum, Copenhagen, Denmark)

neighbouring principality of Polotsk in an effort to strengthen this southern neighbour. His primary concern was, however, the Mongols. Isolated and vulnerable, Alexandre's principality of Novgorod had little choice but to submit and make these eastern conquerors into allies against western aggression.

In fact, Alexandre Nevskii was following the same policy as the Byzantine Emperor of Nicea, far to the south, under similar threat from Crusader aggression. Both preferred the religious toleration of the Mongols to the anti-Orthodox persecution of the Catholics, and both realised that the Mongols were here to stay.

Alexandre's loyalty was soon rewarded: the Mongol Khan permitted him to become *Veliki Knez* of Russia in 1252, and he retained that title until his death. Alexandre's influence lasted longer, as the Russian historian H. Paszkiewicz wrote in the 1950s: *"Alexander Nevsky was, undoubtedly, the most remarkable personality amongst the sons of Yaroslav. Following his father's example, he endeavoured to provide his sons with as large an inheritance as possible. Two of these sons – Dimitri and Andrew – engaged in an embittered conflict for the Grand-Ducal throne. . . . The third son of Alexander,*

ALEXANDRE NEVSKII

Alexandre Nevskii, his wife, his mother and his *druzhina* military following were driven out of Novgorod during the winter of 1240/41 for unknown reasons. Whether they were urged on their way by one of the city's *skomorokhi* minstrels is unknown. These strange figures are said to have been descended from the pagan priests of ancient Russia and they played an important role among the still barely Christian poorer people.

Danilo (d.1303), never obtained Grand-Ducal dignity but deserves our attention on account of the growing strength of the principality held by him, which was none other than Moscow."

Alexandre's younger brother Andrey Yaroslavich was equally warlike but less astute. The importance of his role at the battle of Lake Peipus remains unclear, though it was emphasised by the writer of the *Suzdal Chronicle* (Andrey being ruler of Suzdal): *"Grand Prince Yaroslav sent his son Andrey to Novgorod the Great to help Alexandre against the Germans and they defeated them beyond Pskov on the lake and took many prisoners. And Andrey returned to his father with honour."*

Nothing is known of Andrey's early days, and his entire life is confused by contradictory sources. As well as ruling Suzdal, he may have had hereditary rights over the small towns of Gorodec and Nizni Novgorod, which were given him by his father, Yaroslav. After the battle of Lake Peipus, Andrey seized the city of Vladimir, along with the title of Grand Prince, then took part in the only concerted effort to resist the Mongol occupation. But this alliance with Mikhail of Chernigov and Andrey's father-in-law, Daniil of Galich, and Volhynia was easily crushed

in 1252, after which Andrey fled to Sweden. The Mongols permitted him to return when he submitted to his brother, Alexandre of Novgorod, who in turn allowed Andrey to reclaim the city of Suzdal, where he ruled until his death.

Another interesting but far less important Russian leader was Domash Tverdislavich. Nothing is known of him except that he was the brother of Novgorod's *posadnik* and was killed by Crusader forces in a minor skirmish shortly before the battle of Lake Peipus. Yet quite a lot can be deduced from this alone. The Tverdislav family had been supporters of Yaroslav Vsevolodovich for some time. They were not of princely rank, but were probably *boyars* of Novgorod or the surrounding area. Stepan Tverdislavich was the son of a former *posadnik* (mayor) of Novgorod. He then emerged as a leader of the riots which ousted the then *posadnik*, an opponent of the Vsevolodovich cause, in 1230. Stepan was himself proclaimed *posadnik* later that year and he remained a loyal ally of Yaroslav and his son Alexandre Nevskii until his death in 1243. His brother, Domash Tverdislavich, was *tysyatskiy*, or commander of Novgorod's own militia.

ABOVE **The Bamberg Rider is one of the finest examples of medieval sculpture, and was made around 1230. Though the horseman himself wears civilian clothing, his saddle and the rest of the horse's harness is the same as that used in war. (*in situ* Cathedral, Bamberg, Germany)**

LEFT **Wall painting showing Prince Yaroslav Vsevolodovich, father of Alexandre Nevskii, offering the Church of the Saviour to Christ, c.1246. The painting was made when Alexandre Nevskii ruled Novgorod. (*in situ*, Church of the Saviour, Nereditsa, Russia)**

RIGHT **Central panel of a Russian icon illustrating the life of Saint George, made in Novgorod early in the 14th century. (inv. 2118, Russian Museum, St. Petersburg, Russia)**

ГЕОРГЕН
АГИОСЬ
ГРА
ДЬГЬ
КЛН

NATIVE PEOPLES OF NORTH-EASTERN EUROPE – c.1242

0   100   200 Miles
0   100   200   300 Km

N

Finno-Ugrians
Balts
Slavs
Germanic
Turkic
— · — Political frontiers
— — Approximate linguistic-
        tribal boundaries

(Pagans)   Saami/Lapps

Saami/Lapps

NORWAY

Scandinavians

Saami/Lapps

(Pagans)

Samoyeds

SWEDEN

Suomi

Swedes

Emi

Karelians

Ves

BALTIC
SEA   Osilians

Danes

Ests   Vod   Izhora

NOVGOROD

ROSTOV

CRUSADER
LUVONIA

Curonians

Livs

Merya

Kursi

Semigallians   Lettigallians-
                       Selonians

PEREYASLAVL   YURIEV

Teutonic
Knights   Samogitians

Zhemaitui

Prussians

Aukshtaitui

Lithuanians
(Pagans)

SMOLENSK

Meshera

POLOTSK

Areas of heavy
German
Colonization

Yatvyagi

Slavs

POLISH
STATES

CHERNIGOV

MUROM-
RYAYAN

TUROV-
PINSK

Areas of heavy
German
Colonization

VOLHYNIA

NOVGOROD-
SEVERSK

KIEV

Turks
Mongols

GALICH   PEREYASLAVL

OPPOSING FORCES

CRUSADER ARMIES: RECRUITMENT

Apart from large numbers of local Estonian and Balt auxiliaries, the armies of Crusader Livonia and Danish northern Estonia mirrored those of northern Germany and Denmark. They consisted of the Military Orders, though only the Teutonic Knights existed by 1242, plus the secular settler vassals with their retinues and the urban settler militias. These forces could sometimes rely on Crusaders from outside, who came for one season's campaign, usually in response to a wave of preaching in Germany.

The feudal system of structuring society came late to Germany, particularly to the eastern borderlands. The essentially French concept of knighthood was also late in reaching Germany, developing in the 12th century when a knightly class evolved out of minor military vassals and legally 'unfree' *ministeriales*. They came to be rated as noblemen by the late 12th century in a social, if not strictly legal, manner. By the 13th century many '*ministerial*' families were acting like independent robber-barons, looting, stealing and fighting private wars with other *ministeriales*. The term '*riter*', which originally meant a servant, came to mean 'knight', while the term '*knecht*', which similarly indicated a servant or valet, also rose in military prestige during the 13th century.

In fact the '*ministerial*' class formed the recruiting base of the German crusading Military Orders. Joining any Military Order entailed less 'abandoning of the world' than did entering a monastery. Members of the Military Orders were expected to be less well educated than monks and this, along with their shedding of human blood, gave them less religious status. By the 13th century, however, the Military Orders were widely seen as the best part of a Church that was in disarray.

Motives for joining were not always idealistic. Some recruits escaped domestic problems in return for high military prestige and regular meals. Even so there was a pecking order among the Military Orders: the Sword Brethren were a second–class Order compared to the Templars, Hospitallers and Teutonic Knights. Its brother knights largely came from the poorer end of the *ministerial* class, and even before the disastrous battle of Saule river the Sword Brethren only numbered around 110 brother knights, 400–500 mounted sergeants, 700 assorted mercenaries, 400 secular German vassals and up to 5,000 native auxiliaries.

As always the brother knights formed a tiny military elite within the overall establishment. Half of the organisation survived to be incorporated into the Teutonic Knights, and they provided the bulk of the latter's contribution to the Novgorod Crusade. Beneath the brother knights, the servants of both the Sword Brethren and the Teutonic Knights formed separate branches: professional infantry and cavalry,

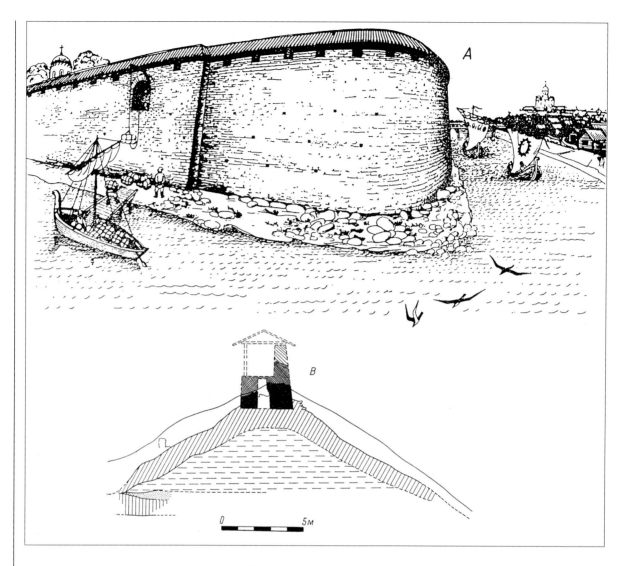

A

B

0   5м

The original medieval walls of Pskov were replaced many centuries later, but they probably looked much like the early 12th century fortifications of Old Ladoga, which have been excavated by Russian archaeologists. A: Reconstruction of the northern bastion overlooking the junction of the Volkhov and Ladoga rivers. B: Section through the existing southern wall, showing what was probably a timber superstructure.

non-combatant support personnel, and perhaps auxiliaries from the German settler merchants and nobles of Riga. Around 1225, in fact, the Sword Brethren had requested permission to recruit brother knights from the Rigan middle class; these being acceptable to the *ministeriales* who already formed the Brethren's military elite. The early and mid 13th century Teutonic Knights were similar, though richer and better organised.

The decline of enthusiasm for crusading, which was felt across most of western Europe in the first half of the 13th century, caused even the Teutonic Knights recruitment problems. Most of the brother knights were still of German origin and most joined for religious reasons – namely to atone for sins through personal sacrifice – but this did not prevent them retaining traditional attitudes to warfare. A delight in combat runs through literature of this period, as one poem celebrating a Teutonic Knight's victory over the pagans in 1234 makes plain: "*Let us all show joy of heart, for lo, the heathen feel the smart.*" Baltic crusading warfare could be exceptionally ruthless, with forcible conversion and the extermination of those who resisted. It drew upon the concept of Holy War

drawn up by medieval theologians to deal with the peaceful ethos of Christianity; this in turn relying heavily on the Old Testament's less ambiguous attitude to warfare.

'Seasonal' Crusaders, who often came to Livonia in large numbers, mostly did so in summer. For Germans, crusading in the Baltic was easier and cheaper than going to the Middle East, but it gave less religious merit (full papal indulgences – the wiping out of previous sins – were only offered from 1245). Many men also seem to have gone crusading merely for adventure and booty. Such mixed motives were reflected in the Swedish *Erikskrönikan* chronicle's description of the Finnish Crusade of 1249: *"Their loud lament the ladies sang, and hands most piteously wrang; Yet still rejoiced when out men rode, to magnify the honour of God. And many an old ancestral sword, that long the walls had encumbered, was snatched from the nails where it slumbered . . . And well I trust, those men did win, gold and silver and herds of kine . . . And he who was fain to bow the knee, and go to the font and Christian be; They left him his life and his goods to enjoy, to live in peace, without annoy. But the heathen who still denied Our Lord, they gave him death for his reward."*

A large proportion of the secular vassals who settled in lands ruled by the Danish crown or the Military Orders came from Saxony, and though they continued to live and behave as their ancestors had done, many appear to have lived in the new settler towns, rather than on fiefs surrounded by a sullen indigenous population. In return for their fiefs this settler aristocracy provided military support and other feudal dues to their lords, whether the latter were the Danish crown, the bishops or the Military Orders. Many also recruited mercenaries to garrison their castles and maintained sergeants with control over their own smaller fiefs.

Urban militias played a relatively minor role, but included infantry from the German craftsmen and some cavalry from the richer merchants. Nevertheless, Riga was a sufficiently important source of manpower for there to be fierce competition for recruits between the Bishop of Riga, the Military Orders and the city's governing council.

Indigenous levies recruited from local converts played a more significant role in the 13th and 14th centuries. At first there was a general levy of fighting men, though this was later replaced by a fixed quote of troops from each

The early 14th century carvings round a capital from the Teutonic Knights' castle of Marienburg in northern Poland. It shows members of the Military Order fighting pagan Prussians. Some of the latter wear lamellar armour; one is armed with a recurved Asiatic style bow. (Malbork Castle Museum)

This 13th century bronze aquamanile is thought to be German, but the very simple style, the hunting animal behind the rider's saddle and the fact that similar aquamaniles are found in other parts of Europe might suggest an eastern European origin. (Hermitage Museum, St. Petersburg, Russia)

RIGHT **Moravian manuscript of 1212-1220 illustrating Abraham and Isaac on the upper row, Jacob and Esau on the lower. Abraham carries his sword and travelling supplies in a sack, much as a soldier would on campaign; Esau has a bowcase, which shows the influence of Asiatic archery techniques on eastern and central Europe. (Hours of the Virgin, M.739, f. f.11v, Pierpont Morgan Lib., New York, USA)**

vakus, or district. Such locally recruited Estonians, Finns and Balts provided their own arms and were primarily motivated by the prospect of plunder and rape. Large numbers served as mounted infantry or light cavalry, usually being placed on the flanks of the Military Orders or settler forces in battle. Otherwise their primary role was scouting, foraging and providing labour during siege operations.

Crusader Armies: Organisation

Both the German Military Orders in Livonia were modelled on the Templars. The Teutonic Knights, for example, had clear regulations governing mobilisation, parade, route marches, pitching camp, mounting guard and conduct in battle – almost everything was done in strict silence. The local or provincial marshal was responsible for discipline, and his tent also served as a field chapel if the provincial master was not present. Teutonic Knights' methods of conquest were the same as those already used in the German *Drang Nach Osten*, or conquest of neighbouring Slav territory: each newly acquired district was colonised by secular knights and an urban bourgeoisie acting as the Order's vassals. In Livonia, river boats known as *bolskip* played a major communications and military transport role, linking the otherwise scattered *komtur* administrative districts, each of which was governed by an *advocatus*, or bailiff, based in its main castle.

Little is known of the military organisation of the secular vassals of Livonia and Estonia, but it is again likely to have reflected conditions in Germany and Denmark. In Germany, for example, '*ministerial*' knights

LEFT **Stained glass window showing the *Massacre of the Innocents*, Swedish, 13th century. (From Gotland, inv. nr. 2976:VI:4, Statens Historiska Museum, Stockholm, Sweden)**

31

The helmeted head, shoulders and shoulders and shield of a knight being devoured by a serpent on an early 13th century German carving. (*in situ* Wartburg Castle, Eisenach, Germany)

went to war accompanied by servants who would look after arms, armour and horses. A knight with two or three sergeants and servants may already have been regarded as a *gleven* or 'lance', a military term first seen in early 13th century Germany. A remarkably high degree of organisation had characterised late 10th and 11th century Danish armies, which were in some respects more advanced than most of the rest of Europe. But by the 12th and 13th centuries Danish armies were largely modelled upon those of northern Germany, though a little old fashioned, while Swedish armies were 50 or so years further behind the times.

Indigenous auxiliaries fought under their own 'elders' and in the early 13th century their organisation is likely to have been similar to that of the old pagan armies – known as *karya* in Prussia or *karias* in Lithuania. Whereas Lithuanian and even Estonian leaders rode full-sized war-horses, ordinary warriors only had small ponies, while among the poorer northern Finns only the elite warriors had any form of horse. The *Livonian Rhymed Chronicle* adds the interesting information that while soldiers of German origin maintained morale before battle by playing drums, pipes and other musical instruments, Liv and Lett tribesmen clashed their weapons against their shields.

Crusader Armies: Tactics

Crusader armies in the Baltic used basically the same tactics as other western European armies, though with local variations. A commander's primary offensive aim was to mislead enemy defenders and make them go the wrong way while his own army penetrated and ravaged their territory. Concern to catch the enemy at a disadvantage was mirrored by a fear of being similarly caught. In battle, banners served as means of identification, as rallying points and for rudimentary communications. They

Carved relief illustrating the Massacre of the Innocents, Swedish c.1300. It is interesting to note that the sculptor has given the chief of Herod's soldiers a form of scale or lamellar armour, probably indicating that he is a 'wicked easterner' or an 'infidel'. (*in situ* Cathedral, Linköping, Sweden. Colette Nicolle photograph)

LEFT **Mid 13th century painted wooden panel illustrating the story of Saint Mary of Antioch. Here the guards of governor Olibrius have the simple mail armour, brimmed helmets and large shields characteristic of old fashioned 13th century Scandinavian armies. (*in situ* Torpo stave-church, Ål, Norway. Jo. Sellæg photograph)**

were so important that a *gonfanonier,* or standard-bearer, was liable to severe punishment if he personally struck a blow during the fighting. The Templars always carried folded spare banners in case the first were lost, and the German Military Orders would have done the same.

There are no German military manuals compatible with that of the Templars, but again, German practice is likely to have been similar. For example, great effort was made to keep knights close together in a charge, despite their horses' natural tendency to spread out. A knight was not to leave his place once ranks had been drawn up, and once close combat had started he could not retire even if wounded. Mounted sergeants would usually fight alongside or in immediate support of the knights. In the latter case, their primary function was to keep a victorious enemy at bay while the knights re-formed. Infantry normally fought in a defensive anti-cavalry role, in close-ordered ranks that formed a 'shield wall' armed with spears.

The most distinctive characteristics of Baltic crusading warfare reflected the harsh climate, difficult terrain and the unorthodox tactics used by their pagan foes. Garrisons, for example, soon learned that it was more effective to attack raiders on their way home, slowed down by booty and prisoners. Summer operations tended to be on a larger scale, often employing seasonal Crusaders and relying on river or naval transport. Small-scale Crusader raiding was undertaken in winter by resident troops using frozen rivers and marshes as highways. Such winter operations also led to a heavy loss of horses.

Siege warfare, both offensive and defensive, was so important in the Baltic Crusades that the Sword Brethren were specifically trained in it. It was, in fact, the Crusaders' use of small castles, together with their crossbows and heavy body armour, which gave them their military edge. These first castles were made of timber, using local labour, and even in

Statue of Saint Maurice, German c.1250. This saint was often portrayed as an African. Here he also wears the latest form of German coat-of-plates over his mail hauberk, perhaps indicating that such modern armour was of eastern or even Islamic derivation. (*in situ* Cathedral, Magdeburg, Germany)

the 1250s there were probably only ten stone towers in Livonia, made from pre-cut materials that had been brought by river.

Indigenous Baltic military skills concerned rapid raiding by mounted infantry and the laying of ambushes. Surviving descriptions of such raids make the local warriors sound remarkably like the woodland Indians of North America. The cavalry elite of Estonians and Balts *"rode in the ancient fashion"*, according to their Crusader foes, not using the tall wood-framed war saddles of western knights. Their battle tactics had much in common with those of the Mongols, except that Baltic horsemen used javelins rather than bows. They would charge their enemy, hurl a javelin, then retreat, repeating this until all javelins were spent.

When fighting on foot, the best-armed elite used sword and shield until one side weakened and fled to its nearby horses. In siege warfare such Baltic troops used large mantlets made from new-cut timber supported by curved poles. Native fortifications were made of horizontal logs reinforced by tower-like bastions roofed with bark and plastered with clay. During winter sieges snow was used to douse fires. Under Sword Brethren, and probably also Teutonic Knights, command local infantry auxiliaries normally entered battle ahead of the knights, in a well ordered manner, singing and beating drums to maintain morale.

RUSSIAN ARMIES: RECRUITMENT

The medieval Russian people were a mixture of Slavs, Balts, Finns, Lapps, Scandinavians, Turco-Mongols and others. Its society consisted of free and unfree, with a half-free class somewhere between. The aristocracy and military elite were also of mixed origin, stemming from the old pagan Slav tribal leadership, Scandinavian mercenaries and merchants, a previous Alan (Iranian steppe nomad) ruling class, a subsequent Turkish nomad ruling elite, and various Circassian, eastern Magyar (Hungarian) elites – all of which had been assimilated as 'Russians' by the early 13th century. Many Varangian–Scandinavian warriors on their way to serve in Byzantium had remained in Russia, but this flow had virtually dried up. Nevertheless, soldiers of supposed Varangian descent were found in the *druzhina* military followings of various Russian princes.

The *druzhinas* themselves recruited high ranking men as well as those of humble origin. As such the *druzhina* formed a new aristocracy of service alongside an existing elite based upon land, wealth or tribal support. Together the *druzhinas* and the old aristocracy formed Russia's new *boyar* class. At the same time, the small and poorly developed middle class of medieval Russia formed urban militias such as that of Novgorod. These militias were of limited effectiveness on their own, and so tended to march alongside the *druzhina* of their local *knez*. In dire emergencies the *smerdi*, or peasantry, could be summoned to form a large but notably ineffective levy known as the *voi*.

Like many of the Russian states, Novgorod also ruled over and recruited from a large non-Slav population of Finno-Ugrian peoples. The forest-dwelling Ves to the north-east were the first to be dominated by Novgorod; then came the Korel or Karelians to the north-west. Further afield the Finno-Ugrian Mansi were hunter-gatherers inhabiting the sparse forest zone or *taiga* lying immediately south of the Arctic *tundra*. So too were the Zyrians of the far north-eastern corner of Novgorod's empire. Other peoples of this little-known part of medieval Europe were the Votyaks of the upper Kama river and the ethnically Turco-Mongol Ugri hunters and fishermen who inhabited both sides of the northern Ural mountains. Those of the west, also known as the Khantz, had been incorporated into Novgorod's 'fur empire', while their cousins who roamed the vast swamplands and *taiga* forests of the Ob basin east of the Urals were, as yet, beyond Novgorod's rule.

Militarily more important than these Finno-Ugrians were Turco-Mongol warriors of steppe origin. Their influence on Russian armies was enormous. Since it proved impossible to make Russians into effective, or at least numerous, horse-archers, Russian rulers constantly recruited steppe peoples for this purpose and as herdsmen, to raise the horses needed by the *druzhinas*. The flow of such specialists into Russian territory was helped by a Turco-Mongol tradition whereby the military elites of steppe tribes often migrated west or north if defeated by newcomers from the east, while the bulk of their tribe was absorbed by the conquerors. Various waves of such defeated elites formed the famous *Chernye Klobuki* or 'Black Caps', who played a major military role in the late 12th and early 13th centuries. Most were found in southern Russia, but their fate following the first Mongol invasion is unclear. Like the Kipchaq Turks, who actually ruled the western steppes when the Mongols arrived, they may have fled still further west or north, into central Europe and central Russia. Whether or not any significant numbers of Black Caps and Kipchaqs reached Novgorod remains unknown. Nevertheless, it is possible that Alexandre Nevskii's contingent of horse-archers at the battle of Lake Peipus were such men, rather than Mongols, as has been suggested.

The Kipchaqs themselves were remarkably Europeanised by the time

Carved stone icon of Saint George from northern Russia, c.1250. Though primitive and devoid of Byzantine artistic influence, this portrayal also gives Saint George a western European long-sleeved mail hauberk and a kite-shaped shield, suggesting that the reality of early 13th century military technology in northern Russia was similar to that of neighbouring Scandinavia. (State Russian Museum, St. Petersburg, Russia)

Virtually the same methods of timber construction used in 13th century Russian fortresses are used for some houses in the Russian countryside. This example in Vladimir shows how the tree-trunks were grooved to make a weatherproof fit and to achieve a strong corner. (Author's photograph)

of the Mongol invasion. In 1219 their ruler, Köten Khan, helped *knez* Mstislav of Novgorod retake the south-western Russian state of Galich from the Hungarians, and a few years later the Kipchaqs of what is now Moldova had been converted to Catholic Christianity. In 1239 Köten Khan and part of his people fled the Mongol advance to Hungary. Two years later Köten Khan was murdered by Germans and Austrians, partly because these assassins believed he planned to help the Russians conquer Hungary. Köten Khan's people then fled south before returning after the Mongol whirlwind had passed. But whether any of them fled north into Russian territory remains unknown. However, a Christian named Sangor, whom the European traveller Friar Plano Carpini met around 1246, is unlikely to have been the only Kipchaq member of Alexandre Nevskii's *druzhina*.

If the horse-archers on Alexandre Nevskii's right flank at the battle of Lake Peipus were Mongols rather than Turkish refugees, they would probably have come north with Alexandre's brother Andrey of Suzdal. They are unlikely to have been the military contingent of a Mongol *baskak*, or tax-gatherer, in Novgorod as that city had not yet officially submitted to Mongol rule.

The motivation of Alexandre Nevskii's army was as mixed as that of its Crusader foes. The modern idea that Orthodox eastern Christianity was a peaceful religion compared to Catholic western Christianity is a myth – or was during the Middle Ages. By the 13th century Orthodox Christianity had a militant though not a crusading aspect. Many Orthodox saints were portrayed as soldiers, and Alexandre Nevskii himself had a particular affection for the Russian warriors Saints Boris and Gleb. Russian rulers tended to have themselves portrayed in Byzantine imperial style, while the aristocratic literature of the period is just as warlike as its western counterparts. The *Epic of Prince Igor* is said to have been written shortly before the Novgorod Crusade, though the existing version clearly includes post-Mongol elements. But it does reflect the ideology of the typical *druzhina*: "*My men of Kursk are glorious warriors, swaddled under trumpets, cradled under helmets, nursed at the spear's point, To them the roads are known and the ravines are familiar, Bent are their bows, open their quivers, sharpened their swords . . . The sons of Rus have barred the great plains with their scarlet shields, seeking honour for themselves and glory*

Fragment of a large carved wooden disc illustrating warriors with swords, kite-shaped shields and pointed caps or helmets. Unlike most Byzantine-style religious art in medieval Russia, this rare example of a 12th century secular decoration suggests that ordinary Russian costume, arms and armour were similar to that of neighbouring western and northern European countries. (Kremlin Museum, Novgorod, Russia)

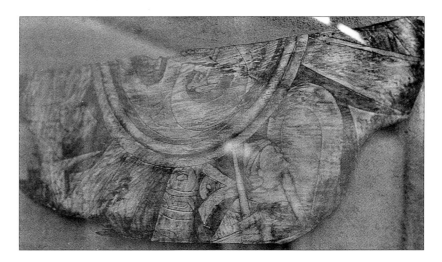

for the prince . . . No longer do I see at the helm my brother Yaroslav, strong, rich and mighty in warriors, with his Chernigov boyars, his valiant druzhina, with the Tatrans and Shelbirs and Topchaks and Revugs and Olbers [various tribal contingents], *without shields, only knife-blade in bootleg, with war-whoops they vanquish hosts, sounding the glory of their grandsires."*

Despite a fierce attachment to the Orthodox church, medieval Russia was also characterised by survivals from its pagan past. This was even seen among the educated ruling elite where, for example, the *postrig* or ceremonial cutting of a boy's hair around the age of four or five was basically a pagan initiation ceremony. Beliefs concerning metallurgy and weapons making included myths linked to the old pagan Slav god Svarog, 'god of white light', while the importance of 'spirit protector' animals such as swans and geese among Slavs and Finno-Ugrians accounts for their persistence in Russian folk legend. The importance of the bear must also have accounted for the use of its name in various Finn settlements, ranging from the Merya tribal town of Medved or 'Bear' in the Kalinin area to the old Estonian name Medvezhya Golova or 'Bear's Head' for the Crusader castle of Otepää near Tartu.

Subsidiary figure of the warrior Saint George, on an icon of Saint Climacus made in Novgorod 1250-1300. (inv. 2774, Russian Museum, St. Petersburg, Russia)

Russian Armies: Organisation

During the 12th and 13th centuries Russia was a melting pot of eastern and western military systems. Ancient infantry traditions survived, but Russian cavalry had also developed in the 10th century in response to the threat posed by steppe civilisations to the south. This included a large number of light cavalry, including some horse-archers drawn either from the steppe nomads themselves or from steppe influenced borderland Russians. During the 12th and 13th centuries a disciplined cavalry elite was modelled on that of the Byzantine army, armed with close-quarter weapons. Even so cavalry as a whole was more typical of southern and perhaps central Russian states than of northern Novgorod.

Armies of the states of Kievan Russia were generally in three parts: the princely *druzhina*; urban militias that had largely replaced the old Russian tribal levies; and assorted non-Slav auxiliary or allied contingents. The *druzhina* itself evolved as a result of wars with the steppe nomads. Bound by oaths of loyalty to its *knez*, the *druzhina* was highly mobile, well trained and well equipped. Two levels of *druzhina* developed in the 11th century: a senior *druzhina* comparable to the 'household' of a western European prince, and a junior *druzhina* consisting of armed retainers. The distinction between senior and junior steadily became more pronounced, but the old concept of a free association remained, whereby a *druzhina*'s members could leave if they wished. In fact the *knez* retained their loyalty only as a result of his own personality and success.

The *voyevoda*, or army commander, was normally selected from the *druzhina*, though he might be the *tysyatskiy* ('commander of a thousand') who led an urban militia. In fact the functions of *tysyatskiy* and *voyevoda* eventually merged. The structure of these militias reflected that of the earlier tribal levies, sometimes even including *sotnia* units – supposedly of 100 men led by a *sotnik*. Membership of the militia was often virtually synonymous with the *veche*, or town assembly. In Novgorod the *veche* was a governing council elected by a general assembly which left everyday administration in the hands of the church, the merchant elite and the *knez*'s representatives. The *posadnik* (mayor) was, however, elected by the *veche* from among the *boyars*. His power depended on circumstances, and could be considerable. The *veche* also chose the city's *tysyatskiy*, who acted as a chief of police as well as militia leader.

The military organisation of Novgorod's tribal auxiliaries, like those of other Russian states, is unknown, but it is likely to have been rudimentary. Perhaps it was structured around Novgorod's *pogost*, or tiny administrative settlements for some of the more primitive native peoples, like the Lapps and Karelians, who had no military elite of their own.

Communications were of paramount importance in a vast country like Russia. During the 12th and 13th centuries armies lived off the land with only the most elementary commissariat of wagons to carry weaponry and essential supplies. In the northern forests the great wagons of the steppes were useless, and everywhere rain and mud made spring and autumn the seasons of *rasputitsa* ('roadlessness'). In fact communications were easier in winter than summer, for when the rivers froze, they formed highways for sledges. In summer the rivers still formed the main arteries of communication, though rapids and cataracts made frequent portages necessary. Russian princes did what they could to improve things by building wooden bridges (though these were easily damaged by floating ice during the spring thaw) and by paving portages with timber. Rulers also offered military protection for the most important portages. In the north there were even efforts to improve rivers by digging canals and removing large rocks.

The little information available about medieval Russian battlefield

Russian manuscript illustration of King David and his usurper son, Absolom, dating from around 1270. This Simonov-Chludov Psalter includes detailed portrayals of the elite warriors of 13th century Russia. Here, for example, Absolom's guards wear a mixture of mail and lamellar armour, showing strong Byzantine and Turco-Mongol influence. (Location unknown)

communications again suggests strong steppe influence. The *Prince Igor* epic describes its hero's banner as having a white flag on a scarlet staff with a Central Asian red-dyed horsetail fluttering from its silver socket. According to the *Livonian Rhymed Chronicle*, an early 13th century Russian army used drums and fifes to rally after a retreat or after crossing a river.

Russian Armies: Tactics

Russian tactics evolved in response to the challenge from the steppes, and while strategy often involved daring offensive operations, battlefield tactics tended to be defensive. Faced by more mobile foes, Russian commanders usually found a position with natural obstacles such as a river or forest to their rear and flanks. (Alexandre Nevskii would also adopt a strong defensive position on the shore of Lake Peipus.) The classic late 12th century Kievan formation, for example, was said to have the cavalry on the flanks with *voi* (infantry) at the centre and *kopejshchik* (spearmen) forming a protective shield-wall for the *luchnik* or *strelets* (archers).

The importance of passive defence is reflected in the *Prince Igor* epic: *"O Vsevolod, furious bison! You stand on the defence, you pour your arrows upon the foemen, you batter their helmets with swords of Frankish steel."*

Russian princes tended to use urban militias to blunt an enemy assault and preserve their elite *druzhina*. The importance of the right flank, which would become so obvious at Lake Peipus, was based upon shamanistic pagan beliefs as well as the medieval infantry's habitual vulnerability to attacks on its left flank.

The question of Russian archery in the pre-Mongol period remains unclear. It is generally thought to have been provided by infantry fighting either in ordered ranks or as skirmishers and by Turkish allies or auxiliaries. But even in 1218 Russian archery was greatly feared by the Livonian levies – and the number of Turks in Novgorod must have been very small at that early date. Meanwhile the big increase in Russian horse-archery came after the Mongol conquest of the mid 13th century.

Siege warfare was not as advanced in 13th century Russia as it was in the west. It had developed in response to different circumstances, most obviously along the southern frontier. Russian *gorodishche* forts were built here and in the east as bases for defence and for expansion into Turkish steppe and Finn forest territory. These fortresses tended to be simple, built of wood rather than stone. Elsewhere a mixture of stone, timber and clay was used.

Timber architecture also differed in Novgorod, which relied on the straight coniferous trees of the north rather than the gnarled deciduous trees of the south. Despite being by far the most important city in northern Russia, Novgorod only had a wooden wall until the existing impressive brick fortifications were erected in the late 15th century. Pskov, on the other hand, had stone defences since the 10th or 11th century. These were later replaced by the existing walls, but may have

Russian embossed silver icon of saints Peter and Paul, 12th century. The military equipment shown in this source is in the pseudo-Roman style of Byzantine art and does not reflect the reality of Russia, nor probably of Byzantium. (Kremlin Museum, Novgorod, Russia)

СТГ ГЕРГИА БЕ...
СБАЗАБЪШКЕ...

The arrest of Saint George, on a Russian icon illustrating the Life of St. George, made in Novgorod early in the 14th century. (inv. 2118, Russian Museum, St. Petersburg, Russia)

been similar to the early 12th century stone fortifications of Old Ladoga, north of Novgorod.

Surviving evidence indicates that even the Lithuanians, the most advanced of the Balt and Finnish peoples, relied on cautious tactics when facing the Crusader or Russian foes. The *Livonian Rhymed Chronicle*, for example, grimly described the pagans' defeat of the Sword Brethren at the battle of Saule: *"More heathens arrived. The next day the Christians thought to ride away early, but they had to fight the pagans though they did not want to. In the swamp they could offer but weak resistance, and they were cut down like women. I lament the deaths of so many heroes who were so easily slain... The Master and his Brothers put up a heroic defence until their horses were slain and even then they fought on foot and felled many men before they were vanquished . . . Finally, and with great difficulty, the Lithuanians felled them with long spears."*

In complete contrast the steppe peoples could draw upon a highly sophisticated and varied military heritage. The Kipchaq army, for example, included both armoured cavalry and lighter horse-archers. They would certainly have used the same shower-shooting tactics as those of their Mongol successors, as so vividly described by Friar Carpini: *"A number of them, each supplied with several quivers complete with arrows, begin to shoot before their opponents' arrows can reach them, sometimes even ahead of time when they are not in range. As soon as their arrows can reach the mark unhindered they are said, owing to the density of their shooting, to rain arrows rather than to shoot them."*

THE SIZE OF THE ARMIES

The Bishop of Tartu's local militia consisted of 300 vassal knights and sergeants and 1,000 or so Estonian auxiliaries. The eastern part of Danish Estonia, to the north of Bishop Hermann's territory, could have raised a militia of around 200 knights and sergeants, plus native auxiliaries, while the Teutonic Knights in what is now Estonia numbered about 350 knights and sergeants plus Estonian auxiliaries. The battle of Lake Peipus, however, involved only part of this total, largely Bishop Hermann's forces. In fact the Crusaders probably totalled around 800 German and Danish knights and sergeants, of whom only a fraction would have been Teutonic Knights, plus some 1,000 Estonians.

The size of the Russian force is much harder to determine. It clearly included Alexandre Nevskii's own *druzhina* and that of the brother Andrey. Their role was comparable to that of the knights on the Crusader side. But a large part of the Novgorod militia was also present, along with Finno-Ugrian tribal contingents, comparable to the opposing Estonian native auxiliaries. The size of the vital Turco-Mongol contingent of horse-archers is unknown, as is their precise identity, but it is unlikely to have exceeded a few hundred. A total of between 6,000 and 7,000 is accepted by most historians, though even this seems excessive. The sizes of the elite or professional forces engaged was probably similar on both sides. Nevertheless, it is clear that the total number of Russians and their allies substantially outnumbered the totality of Crusaders and their auxiliaries.

A battle between King David's army and that of Absolom in the Simonov-Chludov Psalter, late 13th century. (Location unknown)

OPPOSING PLANS

RUSSIAN PLANS

Alexandre Nevskii's overriding concern during the campaigns of 1240–42 was to defend Novgorodian territory by dealing with three Crusader invasions separately and then by launching a limited counter-attack to deter further aggression. Since the battle of Lake Peipus happened almost by accident, there was little in the way of

ABOVE **The massacre of the Innocents and the resurrection of Jesus on an embossed and gilded altar front from Norway, 1225-1250. (*in situ*, Odder Church near Arhus, Norway. Ian Peirce photograph)**

LEFT **A: Plan of the hilltop fortification outside Izborsk, known as Truvor's farmstead. It was built in the 8th-9th century, but the site is now only occupied by a medieval church.**
B: Plan of the fortress at Koporye. The existing walls largely date from the 15th century and remnants of the 13th century Crusader castle were probably incorporated into the massive citadel at one end of the fortress.

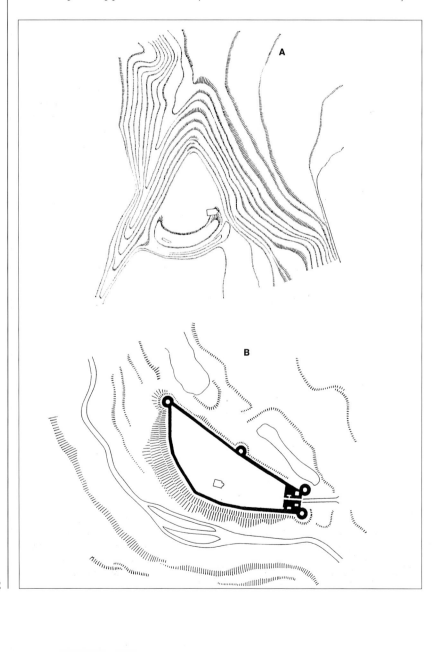

The 15th century walls of Novgorod and the 12th century cathedral within, seen in March. (Author's photograph)

planning. Alexandre Nevskii had raided west of the lake to punish the Latin Crusaders for their invasion and occupation of Russian territory and to follow up his eviction of the Teutonic Knights' garrison from Pskov. There was clearly no intention of occupying Latin territory – he merely wanted to demonstrate his power and inhibit any future attacks on Pskov or Novgorod. This was fully within Russian military traditions of that period.

The fact that Alexandre divided his forces once inside the territory of Hermann, Bishop of Tartu, showed that he intended to inflict as much damage as possible. But in so doing he made them vulnerable to ambush which in turn led to the bruising defeat of one Russian detachment. Alexandre's decision to then regroup and retreat as fast as possible across frozen marshland and the frozen surface of Lake Peipus indicates considerable local knowledge. Nevertheless, he was almost cut off and perhaps forced to fight on the far shore of the lake. In the subsequent battle Alexandre seems to have relied on traditional tactics with a con-

An early 13th century German carving showing an infantry warrior and two fabulous beasts armed with infantry weapons. (*in situ* Cathedral, Frieburg, Germany)

43

siderable emphasis on infantry, though with the somewhat mysterious addition of horse-archers, whose flank attack upon the advancing Crusader army brought victory. Alexandre's unwillingness to follow up this success, even by raiding Crusader territory, reinforces the view that his overall aims were defensive. Nevskii's primary concerns, of course, lay to the south and east, where the Mongol invaders had yet to consolidate their conquest of most Russian states, and with whom Alexandre had yet to reach a stable relationship. For the Russians the battle of Lake Peipus, like the entire Novgorod Crusade, remained a sideshow.

CRUSADER PLANS

Crusader plans showed considerable forethought and were much more ambitious than those of the Russians. Three separate thrusts into Novgorod territory made strategic sense, dividing Russian defences and blocking the main western trading outlets upon which Novgorod depended for its existence. They also avoided too much clash of interests on the Crusader side, since the Swedes would extend their existing conquests in Finland, the Danes their occupation of northern Estonia, and the Teutonic Knights and Bishop Hermann of Tartu their new position in southern Estonia. The individual defeat of each invasion reflected inadequate military strength and an underestimation of Novgorod's resources, miscalculating the degree of help Novgorod would receive from other parts of Russia.

Once these thrusts had been repulsed, the Crusaders seemed paralysed, probably because the Novgorod Crusade project itself had been controversial from the start. The speed of Alexandre Nevskii's retaliatory raid should not have caught the Crusaders by surprise, since it was

A figure representing Master Abraham, the Russian craftsman who assembled the mid 12th century bronze panels of the Magdeburg Doors in Novgorod Cathedral. All the panels except this one were imported from Germany. Nevertheless, Abraham's own appearance and costume differ only slightly from that of the other figures on the doors. (*In situ* Cathedral of Santa Sophia, Novgorod, Russia)

within their own military experience as well as that of the Russians. Nevertheless, local forces responded rapidly, defeating part of the Russian army and obliging the rest to retreat.

The fact that the Crusaders were then able to catch Alexandre Nevskii and force him to fight also demonstrates an ability to move fast over the frozen landscape. In the subsequent battle the Crusader commander adopted standard tactics by making a heavy cavalry charge in close formation with lightly equipped native auxiliaries playing a subordinate role. This charge failed as a result of two factors: an inferiority in numbers, which should have been counterbalanced by the Crusaders' heavier equipment, and, more importantly, by the unexpected presence of horse-archers in the Russian ranks.

ABOVE LEFT AND RIGHT **Carved head of Saint Maurice, patron saint of Bamberg, originally from the main bridge, c.1235. The warrior saint has a remarkably primitive helmet for the time this carving was made, perhaps because the sculptor was trying to make the figure look 'old fashioned'. (Historical Museum, Bamberg, Germany)**

The mid 15th century northern tower of Koporye castle. Any remnants of the 13th century Crusader fortifications would be incorporated into this structure.

LIVONIAN CAMPAIGNS OF 1241–1242

0   50   100 Miles
0   100   200 Km

N

(Pagans)

Lake Ladoga

(Swedes)

† Abo

Battle of River Neva, 1240

Ladoga

Koporye

Swedes, 1240

Tallinn (Reval)
ROTALIA

(Danes)

WIERLAND

Narva

Retaking of Koporye, 1241

Tesov

JERWAN

Danes & Crusaders, 1241

Novgorod

HARRIEN

Battle of Lake Peipus, 1242

SONNTAGIA

Fellin

Tartu (Dorpat) †

NOVGOROD

BALTIC SEA

OESEL

Bishop Hermann, 1242

UNGANNIA

Izborsk

Rusa

SACCALLIA

Liberation of Pskov, 1242

LETTGALLIA

Crusaders, 1241

Pskov

Kamno

CRUSADER LIVONIA

Veukieluki

KURLAND

† Riga

SEMGALLIA

SELONIA

NALSEN

Usvyat

SAMOGITHIA

Polotsk

Vitebsk

(Pagans)

Vilna

POLOTSK

Drutsk

Balga

Teutonic Knights

Logozhsk

Minsk

Izyaslavl

SMOLENSK

POLISH MAYOVIA

VOLHYNIA

TUROV-PINSK

CHERNIGOV

Legend:
- Under Latin/Catholic rule
- Under Orthodox/Russian rule
- Pagan ruled
- → Movement of Crusader Forces
- → Movement of Alexandre Nevski's forces
- ● City or major town
- † Catholic Bishopric
- Crusader or Scandinavian castle
- –·– Frontiers
- OESEL Provinces of Livonia

UNITY THROUGH CRUSADE?

Afew historians deny that there was a Crusade against Novgorod in the sense of a co-ordinated western threat, but those who lived at the time seem to have believed there was. According to the *Holsteinische Reimchronik* the Count of Holstein was among the first to take the Cross: *"In 1239 God's Word came to him as I shall describe. The honourable Count decided upon a great venture. He wanted to do it for his soul's sake. He had to sail. Therefore he called on his son-in-law, Abel, to rule Holstein and all its people . . . His countess went with him to that pious land. Her name was Hedwig. They went to Livonia for the first time, where they suffered much, just as they would have in the Holy Land."*

The Catholic Church also saw the military weakness and political divisions within Novgorod, but justified its aggression on the grounds that Orthodox Russians did little to convert Baltic pagans. Meanwhile the Pope was upset by squabbling among the northern Crusaders, and he probably thought that a joint offensive against Orthodox 'schismatics'

RIGHT **The combat and reconciliation of Parzival and Feirefiz in a German manuscript of c.1250. Parzival's sword has broken on Feirefiz's flat-topped great helm. (Ms. Germ. 19, f. 49v, Bayerisches Staatsbibliothek, Munich, Germany)**

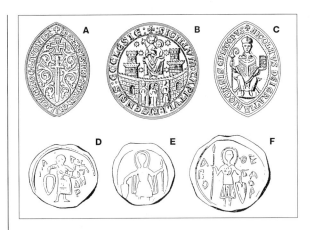

ABOVE **A: Seal of the Military Order of Sword Brethren (1221-32).**
B: Seal of Riga Cathedral (1234-69).
C: Seal of Bishop Nikolaus of Riga (1229-53).
D: Russian princely seal (1236-63).
E: Russian princely seal (1215-36).
F: Russian princely seal (1264-71).

would unify them in a common cause. A truce between the Crusaders and the pagan Lithuanians also left the former free to concentrate on Novgorod. In 1237 Pope Gregory chose William of Modena to organise the Crusade, but although the papacy may have known that Russian attention was focused on the Mongol threat, it cannot have foreseen that the Mongols would launch their great offensive in 1239.

Meanwhile William of Modena journeyed around northern Europe, bringing the major players together. In 1238 he met Hermann Balke of the Teutonic Knights and King Waldemar of Denmark on a Danish island to sign the Treaty of Stensby, settling outstanding disputes. The Teutonic Knights returned much of Estonia to the Danes but retained enough, they hoped, to satisfy the ex-Sword Brethren within their ranks. Meanwhile the turbulent settler nobility in Estonia fought among themselves until the survivors agreed to form knightly corporations to secure their new privileges.

Each of those who took part in the Crusade had their own motives. The Swedes were the most straightforward since they merely wanted to stop Russian missionaries converting eastern Finland to Orthodox Christianity and thus drawing it into Novgorod's orbit. Estonian records suggest that the Danish king and his new vassals in Estonia were the prime movers. Certainly the largely German settler-knights of Estonia

RIGHT **A: Reconstruction of a typical fortified Russian outpost in the 12th/early 13th century. B: Reconstruction of a section through a typical Russian earth and timber fortification of the 11th-12th century.**

A

B

LEFT **Massacre of the Innocents, on the cover of the Great Baptismal Font, German metalwork c.1230. Herod's soldier has again been given scale armour around his waist, apparently to make him look foreign or 'infidel'. (in situ Cathedral, Hildesheim, Germany. Ian Peirce photograph)**

hesitated to offer fealty to an unfriendly Danish ruler or to obey his Bishop of Tallinn. In fact they were probably only won over by promises of lands in Russia.

Bishop Hermann of Tartu had his own ambitions, but not surprisingly the *Livonian Rhymed Chronicle* presented his motives as those of a loyal churchman: *"Bishop Hermann of Dorpat (Tartu) began to quarrel with the Russians in this period. They wanted to obstruct Christianity just as before, and their godlessness caused much harm. They did great mischief, and after he had borne that for a long time he called on the Brothers* [Teutonic Knights] *for help."*

As for the Military Orders themselves, those surviving Sword Brethren who had been unwillingly incorporated into the Teutonic Knights must have played a significant role in promoting the Crusade. It was, after all, in line with previous Sword Brethren ambitions but ran counter to existing Teutonic Knights policy. Over half the Sword **49**

Danish and German
Crusaders building the stone
tower at the existing Vod
tribal settlement of Koporye
in 1241. Most of the labour
would have been done by
local tribesmen; the building
materials were probably
brought up river by barge.
This was the first stone
fortress in the area and it
posed a significant threat to
Novgorodian control of the
southern side of the Gulf of
Finland.

Brethren survived the disaster at Saule, and they remained an influential group. Perhaps they refused to be incorporated into a rival Military Order unless their demand for a continued thrust eastward was accepted. Perhaps the Teutonic Order's leadership agreed in the hope that control of Novgorod would strengthen them in their war against the Lithuanians.

All participants must have hoped that 'pro-western' groups within Novgorod and Pskov would make the campaign easy. Bishop Hermann's brother Theodoric's marriage into a family which had once ruled Pskov had failed to achieve anything, but the Bishop's new brother-in-law, Yaroslav, son of Vladimir Mstislavich, was currently in exile in Livonia seeking support. Crusader garrisons had been in Pskov before, and perhaps they could soon become permanent.

THE CRUSADER ASSAULT

The Mongol invasion of southern Russia may have been seen by the Crusaders as a heaven-sent opportunity to take over northern Russian. Yaroslav Vladimirovich Mstislavich, the exiled and supposedly 'pro-Crusader' *knez* of Pskov, still had supporters at home and in Novgorod, where a so-called 'pro-Nemtsy' party may even have encouraged the Swedish invasion. Dietrich Von Grüningen, Landmeister of Prussia and senior Teutonic Knights commander in the Baltic, showed his disapproval by refusing leadership, money and reinforcements, but his assistant, Andreas Von Felben, did take part in early operations. Other ex-Sword Brethren seem to have provided local leadership. These included Rudolf Von Kassel, castellan of Wenden castle and a troublesome opponent of Bishop Albert of Riga in earlier years (nothing else is known about him).

The *Life of Alexandre Nevskii* explained the sudden Crusader invasion in more personal terms, saying that a western knight named Andres – probably meaning Andreas Von Felben – came to see Alexandre and was so impressed that he told the people at home. As a result the "*king of part of Rum, the midnight country that is Sweden*" sent a challenge saying that he intended to conquer Alexandre's land in 1240.

Previous naval attempts to strangle Novgorod's trade outlet to the Baltic had failed, but this new assault was by both land and river. It was led by Earl Karl Birger, an experienced Crusader in Finland, and Bishop Thomas, the English-born canon of Uppsala who supervised missionary work in Finland. The Swedish invasion force included Norwegians and Finns from the Murman, Suomi and Emi tribes. There was also a small contingent of Teutonic Knights, whose absence may actually have delayed the launching of the central and southern invasions.

Back in Novgorod the threat posed by the Swedes to trade and food supplies was obvious, as the *Novgorod Chronicle* made clear: "*The Swedes came with their ruler and with their bishops, and halted on the Neva at the mouth of the Izhora, wishing to take possession of Ladoga, or in one word of Novgorod and the whole Novgorod province.*" While these invaders established a base on the southern bank of the Neva, the merchants of Novgorod forgot their quarrel with Alexandre and hurriedly recalled him and his elite *druzhina*, while local forces kept watch on the Swedes. According to the

Nothing remains above ground of the castle and Bishop's Palace at Tartu, though the earthworks on top of the citadel hill are still visible. The rectangular base of the castle, seen on the right, is now topped by an observatory, while the surrounding earth ramparts are on the left. (Author's photograph)

Life of Alexandre Nevskii, a Christian 'elder' named Boglusich, from the largely pagan Finnish Izhora tribe, was one of those watching from the river. He saw Saints Boris and Gleb sailing noisily up the Neva one sunrise and, not surprisingly, told Alexandre of this vision of the *knez's* own favourite saints. Thus encouraged, Alexandre led an entirely unexpected dawn attack on the enemy camp, overrunning its defences and forcing the Swedes to flee to their boats. The *Novgorod Chronicle* attributed victory to divine support, saying: "*Again the most kind and merciful God, lover of men, preserved and protected us from the foreigners since they* [the Swedes] *laboured in vain without the command of God. For the news came to Novgorod that the Swedes were going towards Ladoga, and Prince Alexandre with the men of Novgorod and Ladoga did not delay at all. He went against them and defeated them by the power of Saint Sophia and the prayers of our Sovereign Lady the Holy Mother of God and eternally Virgin Mary on the 15th day of July* [1240] . . . *And there was a great slaughter of Swedes.*"

The story of Blanchefleur in a mid 13th century German poetic manuscript. The knights in this battle have their great helms painted in heraldic colours. (Ms. Germ. 51, f. 10r, Bayerisches Staatsbibliothek, Munich, Germany)

This was the Crusaders' first taste of Alexandre's ability to move and strike extremely fast. The battle of the river Neva might have been a relatively small affair, yet it was hard fought and Alexandre was said to have personally wounded the Swedish leader in the face. The Russians lost only 20 or so killed, but this included some senior men, while the fact that many enemy dead were found on the far side of the Neva, where none of Alexandre's soldiers had fought, led the chroniclers to believe that an archangel had been helping the Russians. The Swedish thrust was defeated, but as a result the Swedish church was even keener to convert central Finland and thus forestall an Orthodox Russian take-over. Meanwhile Alexandre earned the title of *Nevskii* from his victory on the Neva.

The central Crusader attack along the southern coast of the Gulf of Finland through the lands of the Vod tribe was more serious and more successful, and was regarded as the real beginning of a campaign which culminated in the battle of Lake Peipus. Once again it caught Novgorod by surprise. Following the defeat of the Swedes, the citizens of Novgorod once more quarrelled with Alexandre Nevskii. They probably felt that peaceful trade with the westerners was essential for the city's survival but he was unwilling to accept their demands and retired in a huff 'to Pereyaslavl' along with his mother, wife and *druzhina*. Alexandre is unlikely to have travelled all the way to the southern city of Pereyaslavl, but probably took up residence in the region around Moscow, which at that time formed a northern enclave of Pereyaslavl territory.

For a while it looked as if the so-called 'pro-German' party had won the day, but during the winter of 1240/41, bands of Crusaders raided deep into Novgorod territory along the Luga river, seized the town of Tesov and reached the village of Sablya, 30 kilometres from Novgorod itself. More ominously, invaders consisting of the Teutonic Knights, vassals of the Danish king and native Estonian auxiliaries took the Novgorodian *pogost* and native settlement of Koporye. Furthermore, by April 1241 they had added a stone castle, thus indicating their intention of holding Vod territory permanently. Once again Novgorod was unable to respond adequately on its own, and the *veche* begged Alexandre to return. Meanwhile the Crusaders imposed tribute on the Vod tribe and continued to raid, stealing so many animals that the Russian farmers were unable to plough their fields for the following year's planting.

Worse still was a third Crusader assault south of Lake Peipus. The anonymous author of the *Livonian Rhymed Chronicle,* writing some years after the event, reflected the confidence felt by these invaders as they entered Russian territory early in September: *"The Master came to him* [Bishop

Saint Maurice on a late 13th century Danish painted wooden panel. The saint wears a coat-of-plates over his mail hauberk, showing strong German influence. (*in situ* Lögum Monastery, Denmark)

EXECUTION OF THE TRAITORS
Alexandre's army re-took Crusader-held Koporye in 1241. Alexandre then executed those local Estonian and Vod tribal 'elders' who had co-operated with the invaders, but released the captured Germans and Danes. Here the scene is set inside the remaining Vod fortifications of earth and timber, rather than the new stone-built Crusader tower. Traditional Russian timber fortresses were built in almost exactly the same way.

Hermann] *straightway with many noble heroes, outstanding and bold, and the king's men* [vassals of the Danish crown] *also came with a fine force. Bishop Hermann was well-pleased. With this army they went happily into Russia, and everything went well for them. They came to a castle, named Isborg* [Izborsk] *and their arrival dismayed the garrison. They took the castle by storm and let not a single Russian escape, killing or capturing all the defenders."*

The Crusader army was probably led by Landmeister Andreas Von Felben, who commanded the Teutonic Knights' contingent. The secular vassals from northern Estonia were under the Danish royal princes Canute and Abel, and the vassals of Tartu and local Estonian auxiliaries would have been under Bishop Hermann. The *druzhina* of Yaroslav, the former *knez* of Pskov who had been in exile in Crusader territory, also took part.

The citizens of Pskov were not willing to lose the vital fortress of Izborsk without a struggle. As the *Livonian Rhymed Chronicle* continues: *"Those from Pskov were unhappy about this news. This is the name of a neighbouring town in Russia, whose inhabitants were extremely evil. None of them stayed behind, but rather all participated in the expedition and grimly stormed*

towards Isborg with many bright cuirasses and helmets shining like glass. There were also many crossbowmen among them. When they came upon the Brothers' army [the Teutonic Knights] *they attacked, and the Brothers and the king's men boldly charged towards them. A vicious battle arose. The Germans hacked great wounds and the Russians suffered terribly. Eight hundred of them were killed and fell on the battlefield, which was near Isborg. The others took to flight and were pursued relentlessly almost all the way back to Russia. The Russians urged their horses on with whips and spurs, convinced that all was lost. As they hurried towards home, the way seemed terribly long to them and the woods were filled with the noise of disaster. The Brothers' army went in pursuit and crossed the river with their band of daring warriors."*

This battle took place on 16 September, and though it was a significant victory, the Crusader chronicler's estimate of 800 Russian killed seems exaggerated. According to the *Chronicle of Pskov*, the Russian force only totalled 600 men. However, it did suffer severe casualties, including its commander, the *voyevoda* Gavrilo Gorislavich.

The Crusaders then camped outside Pskov and ravaged the area for a week, burning Orthodox monasteries, books and icons as well as many

The fortified hilltop settlement known as Truvor's Farmstead, outside Izborsk. It dates from the 8th-9th century but may still have been used as a citadel during the Novgorod Crusade of 1240-1242.

villages. Finally the city agreed with those who already favoured coming to terms with the Crusaders. Some leading families handed over children as hostages, and Tverdilo Ivankovich, the *posadnik* (mayor) of Pskov, who appears to have been a supporter of the exiled *knez* Yaroslav Vladimirovich, had the gates opened.

As the *Livonian Rhymed Chronicle* put it: *"The Pskovians were unhappy about their visitors. The Brothers pitched their tents in a field before Pskov, and the Bishop and the King's men also chose a good place to camp. Many knights and squires were called upon to earn their fiefs now, for the army was informed that they should all prepare for battle, and that they were going to storm the city. The Russians were aware that many troops would assault both city and citadel, and since they had grown weary of battle after Isborg, and since they feared further defeat, they submitted to the Order, asking for a truce. A peace was made by which Gerpolk, their king* [actually the *posadnik* Tverdilo Ivankovich], *willingly gave the castle and the good land over to the Teutonic Knights, to be administered by the Master. And so the attack did not take place."*

The Ahja river south of Ahja town in eastern Estonia. When frozen in winter, even such small rivers as this provided easy routes for armies. (Author's photograph)

Other leading Pskovian families could not accept a Catholic takeover and the governorship of the pro-Crusader *posadnik* Tverdilo Ivankovich, so they fled to Novgorod. Two brother knights from the Teutonic Order, along with some sergeants and other troops, were placed in Pskov's citadel or main gate, while Tverdilo Ivankovich's own militia provided the bulk of the garrison. This would prove to be a costly error, as the author of the *Livonian Rhymed Chronicle* realised: *"After the peace was arranged, the army did not tarry long there, but soon broke camp. They were all happy and gave honour to God, thanking Him greatly. When the army was ready they rode away, but they left two Brothers and a small force of Germans there to guard the land. This proved disastrous for them and their rule was of short duration."*

Yet the Crusaders' confidence remained high, particularly as they had heard that Alexandre Nevskii had quarrelled with the people of Novgorod. Though the garrison in Pskov was tiny, the Crusaders probably had 1,000 men in the Izborsk area and 200–300 around Koporye. The invaders' position looked good, for they had already taken large swathes of Novgorod territory north and south of the Gulf of Finland, where a powerful fleet, sent by Bishop Heinrich of Ösel island, was also threatening Russian trade. Meanwhile Bishop Heinrich himself hurried off to Rome, asking Pope Gregory to nominate him as bishop of Russian regions yet to be conquered. The Pope was sufficiently impressed to order the Archbishop of Lund and the other Swedish bishops to tell their knights *"like Moses to buckle a sword upon his thigh... and put on the armour of the Lord"*.

Then a greater crisis suddenly loomed. The Mongols, having crushed Russian resistance, invaded Catholic central Europe. The Crusaders were faced with the dilemma of whether to concentrate on fighting them in Poland, Hungary and eastern Germany or to continue with their thrust into north-western Russia. In broad terms the Crusaders probably expected to offer Russia military assistance against the Mongols, and were conceited enough to dismiss the idea that the Russians might decline. Daniil, ruler of the south-western Russian state of Galich, was already negotiating such assistance, and there were groups in both Pskov

The marsh and river at Mooste in summer. Dense forests still fringe the area where a Russian raiding party was ambushed in 1242. (Author's photograph)

BATTLE OF MOOSTE BRIDGE
The death of Domash
Tverdislavich at the battle of
Mooste bridge, some days before
the final battle on Lake Peipus.
The Russians had been plun-
dering the countryside but were
ambushed by local Crusader and
Estonian defence forces.
Domash himself was probably
commander of the Novgorod city
militia.

and Novgorod with the same idea. Perhaps such an alliance could have succeeded. Meanwhile the combined forces of Crusaders and Pskovian militia were raiding closer to Novgorod.

The Teutonic Knights remained split on the issue. Master Dietrich Von Grüningen in Prussia was primarily concerned with the Mongol threat, as were the Grand Master and Grand Chapter of the Order, while Andreas Von Felben seemed unable to make a clear decision, while at the same time having his hands full with a native rising on Ösel island.

The death of King Waldemar and the return of his sons Canute and Abel to Denmark meant that continued direct Danish involvement in the Novgorod Crusade was unlikely, at least until things settled down under the new king, Eric IV. However, this did not dampen the enthusiasm of ex-Sword Brethren in Teutonic Knights' ranks. Like the disaffected vassals of Danish northern Estonia, they probably saw this as an opportunity to violate the Treaty of Stensby and regain northern Estonia as well as conquering Novgorod.

ALEXANDRE'S RESPONSE

The Crusaders had a second taste of Alexandre Nevskii's Mongol-like ability to strike hard and unexpectedly. The Mongols' decision, earlier in 1241, not to attack Novgorod had left the Russians free to concentrate on the immediate problem of Crusader incursions. By that time the raiders had made damaging inroads. During the spring or summer the *veche* of Novgorod, realising that the city militia could not cope with the Crusaders and their new Pskovian allies on its own, asked Alexandre to return (apparently abandoning the demands which had led to their previous quarrel). Alexandre's father, the *Veliki Knez* Yaroslav Vsevolodovich, at first refused to let Alexandre go, instead offering Novgorod his next son, Andrey, the *knez* of Suzdal. This the Novgorodians refused, and since their city remained the richest trading centre of northern Russia, Yaroslav finally allowed Alexandre and his vital *druzhina* to sail back up the Volga into Novgorodian territory.

On his arrival Alexandre Nevskii took drastic action, hanging many who had previously opposed his rule. He then swiftly led his *druzhina* against Crusader garrisons in the Vod lands along the southern coast of the Gulf of Finland. This second counter-attack took place in the autumn of 1241 and Alexandre's own elite troops formed the spearhead of a larger force of local troops and tribal auxiliaries. Opposition was minimal and the new stone-built Crusader castle of Koporye soon fell. As the *Novgorod Chronicle* made clear, Alexandre's victory was complete and again ruthless: "*Knez Alexandre came to Novgorod and the men of Novgorod rejoiced. The same year Knez Alexandre went with the men of Novgorod, and of Ladoga, and with the Karel and Izhora people against the town of Koporye, against the Nemtsy [Germans and Danes], and took the town and brought some Nemtsy to Novgorod and let others go free. But the Vod and Chud [Estonian] traitors he hanged.*"

The biographical *Life of Alexandre Nevskii* portrayed its hero in a rather more gentle light, stating that he killed some of the garrison, captured the rest, keeping a few for ransom but pardoning others and letting them go, "*for he was merciful beyond measure*". Such behaviour, and

The Russian shore of Lake Peipus, seen from Mehikoorma on the Estonian shore during summer. This is just about the narrowest part of the straits which divide Lake Peipus almost in two. (Author's photograph)

the fact that Alexandre did not go on to attack Crusader territory west of the river Narva, indicated that he was only interested in preserving Novgorodian territory. He may, in fact, still have been concerned about a potential Mongol threat.

Given the speed and effectiveness of Alexandre's moves against Swedes in the north, and Danes and others in the centre, his sudden counter-attack in the south should have come as no surprise to the Crusaders holding Pskov. Yet it did, and no effort seems to have been made to reinforce that tiny garrison of Teutonic Knights. Perhaps the whole idea of a Crusade against Novgorod, which had only received half-hearted support, was now crumbling. Nevertheless, the Crusader presence in Pskov remained a more serious menace than either of the other Latin threats.

This time Alexandre did not act alone, but was supported by his brother Andrey with his professional *druzhina* from Suzdal. Together with the Novgorod militia, the Vsevolodovich brothers headed south-west early in 1242. The fearsome Russian winter was still gripping the countryside, and they probably marched across the frozen marshes which covered much of the land between Novgorod and Pskov. At all events they appeared outside the latter so quickly that there were still only two Teutonic Knight brothers in the garrison, along with sergeants and others from the Military Order and Pskov's own forces. The city fell almost without a struggle on 5 March, before the larger garrison in nearby Izborsk could intervene. The importance of this coup was not lost on the author of the *Novgorod Chronicle*: "*In the year 6750* [1242] *Prince Alexandre went in winter with men from Novgorod and with his brother Andrey with men of the Lower Country* [the middle Volga basin around Suzdal] *in great force to the land of the Chud people* [Estonia] *against the Nemtsy* [Germans] *lest they boast and say; We will humble the tribe of Sloves* [the people of the Novgorod region] *to ourselves. For Pskov had been taken and its tiun* [bailiff] *imprisoned. And Prince Alexandre seized all the roads to Pskov, stormed the city by a sudden attack, and seized the Nemtsy and Chud and binding them in chains, imprisoned them in Novgorod.*"

Both Teutonic Knight brothers were captured, and the collapse of Pskov was seen as a severe blow in Crusader Livonia. The *Livonian Rhymed Chronicle* also indicates that Alexandre was welcomed as a liberator: *"There is a city in Russia called Novgorod, and when its king [Alexandre] heard what had happened he marched towards Pskov with many troops. He arrived there with a mighty force of many Russians to free the Pskovians and these latter heartily rejoiced. When he saw the Germans he did not hesitate long. They drove away the two Brothers, removed them from their governorship and routed their troops. The Germans fled and allowed the land to revert to the Russians. Thus it went for the Teutonic Knights, but if Pskov had been protected it would have benefited Christianity until the end of the world. It is a mistake to take a fair land and fail to occupy it properly. It is deplorable, for the result is sure to be disastrous. The king of Novgorod then returned home."*

ALEXANDRE'S COUNTER-ATTACK

This time Alexandre did continue military operations, raiding deep into Livonia. But here Crusader forces rallied and put up an effective resistance despite the fact that Catholic Christendom was at that moment enduring a devastating Mongol invasion. Contrary to widespread opinion, the Mongols did not actually intend to conquer central or western Europe, in which they had no particular interest. Their assault was designed to punish the Europeans, and above all the Hungarians, for giving refuge to Köten Khan and those of his Kipchaq

An army of German knights at full charge, early 13th century German metal casket. (Cathedral Treasury, Aachen, Germany)

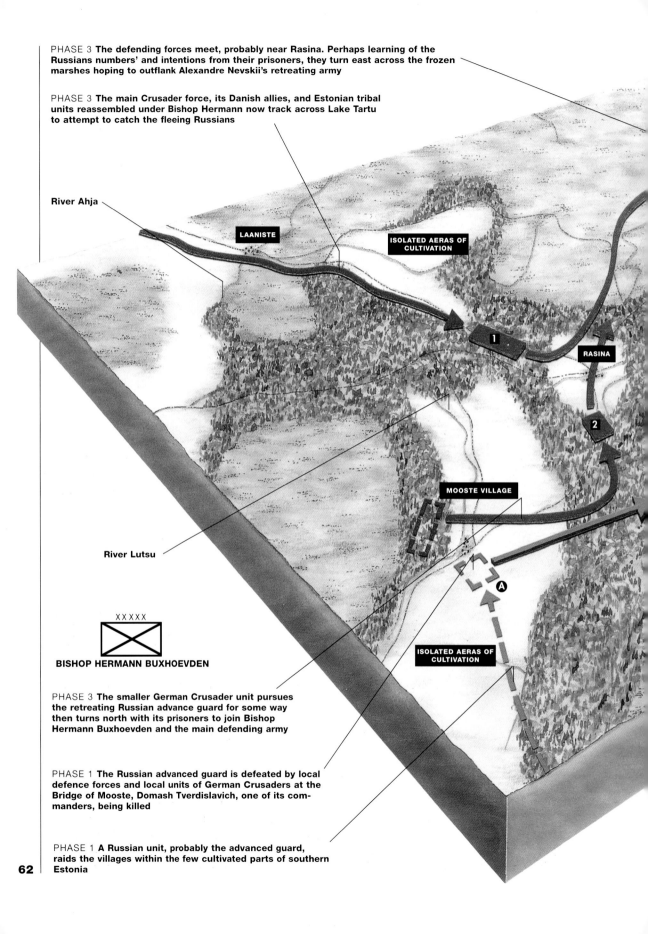

PHASE 3 **The defending forces meet, probably near Rasina. Perhaps learning of the Russians numbers' and intentions from their prisoners, they turn east across the frozen marshes hoping to outflank Alexandre Nevskii's retreating army**

PHASE 3 **The main Crusader force, its Danish allies, and Estonian tribal units reassembled under Bishop Hermann now track across Lake Tartu to attempt to catch the fleeing Russians**

River Ahja

LAANISTE

ISOLATED AERAS OF CULTIVATION

RASINA

1

2

MOOSTE VILLAGE

River Lutsu

XXXXX

BISHOP HERMANN BUXHOEVDEN

A

ISOLATED AERAS OF CULTIVATION

PHASE 3 **The smaller German Crusader unit pursues the retreating Russian advance guard for some way then turns north with its prisoners to join Bishop Hermann Buxhoevden and the main defending army**

PHASE 1 **The Russian advanced guard is defeated by local defence forces and local units of German Crusaders at the Bridge of Mooste, Domash Tverdislavich, one of its commanders, being killed**

PHASE 1 **A Russian unit, probably the advanced guard, raids the villages within the few cultivated parts of southern Estonia**

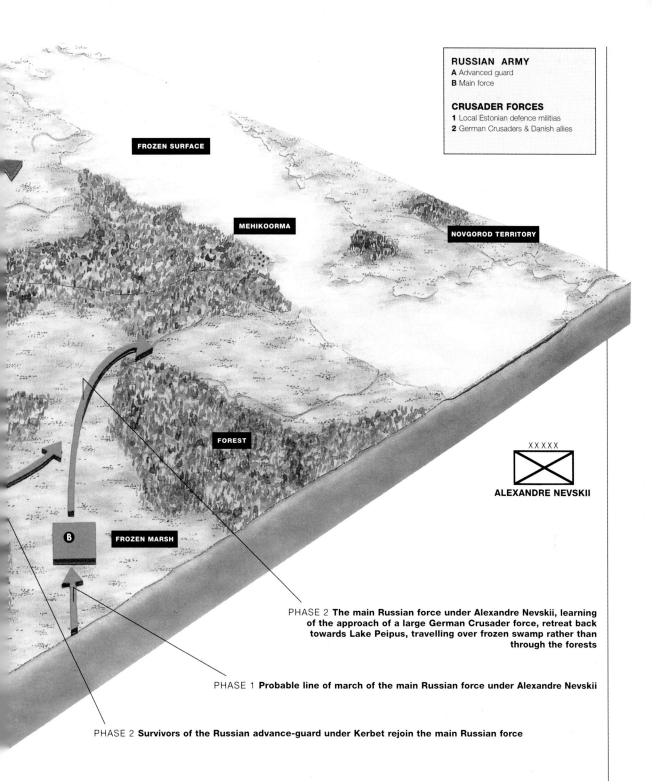

RUSSIAN ARMY
A Advanced guard
B Main force

CRUSADER FORCES
1 Local Estonian defence militias
2 German Crusaders & Danish allies

FROZEN SURFACE

MEHIKOORMA

NOVGOROD TERRITORY

FOREST

XXXXX

ALEXANDRE NEVSKII

B FROZEN MARSH

PHASE 2 **The main Russian force under Alexandre Nevskii, learning
of the approach of a large German Crusader force, retreat back
towards Lake Peipus, travelling over frozen swamp rather than
through the forests**

PHASE 1 **Probable line of march of the main Russian force under Alexandre Nevskii**

PHASE 2 **Survivors of the Russian advance-guard under Kerbet rejoin the main Russian force**

BATTLE OF LAKE PEIPUS 1242

During the last days of March and the first days of April 1242, a Russian force under Prince
Alexandre Nevskii crossed the frontier between Novgorod and Livonian Crusader territory, to
ravage the Catholic diocese of Tartu. But it was obliged to turn back towards Russia when
faced by the combined forces of Bishop Hermann Buxhoevden of Tartu and his local allies

The Estonian shore of Lake Peipus at Meerapalu, with Piirissaar island in the distance on the left and the Russian shore barely visible in the centre. (Author's photograph)

followers who had fled the Mongol Great Khan's rule in what is now the Ukraine. A further paradox lay in the fact that Köten Khan had actually been murdered by the Hungarians' Austrian allies a year earlier. Nevertheless, his people, the Kipchaqs, would have a significant military influence upon Hungary, while those who remained under Mongol rule would come to dominate the Golden Horde which now ruled them.

Of more immediate importance to Christendom were those Mongols who were currently careering around the Russian principality of Galich, Poland, the easternmost fringes of the German Empire, Hungary and the Balkans. Faced with this terrifying, fast-moving, efficient and ruthless foe, Europe tried to organise a Crusade in 1241. There seems to have been a good response in Germany, but such military assistance to the Hungarians had minimal impact. Meanwhile the Pope begged the Teutonic Knights to come south and help in the fight against the Mongols. This was precisely the moment when Alexandre Nevskii chose to make his counter-attack following the recapture of Pskov.

Russians, indigenous Baltic peoples and German Baltic Crusaders habitually campaigned during the depths of winter, when the ice-bound landscape was suitable for the movement of armies, but campaigning in the spring and autumn was almost unheard of. These were seasons of 'roadlessness' when the country could dissolve into a sea of mud and the rivers could be choked with dangerous ice-floes as the thaw set in.

The precise date of the spring thaw could, of course, vary, and it was still late winter when Alexandre launched his counter-offensive. In March 1993, for example, the weather in this part of Russia was mostly grey, dismal and well above freezing. Countryside, roads and towns were drenched in mud and melting slush. A severe snowstorm could then advance across the landscape like a greyish white wall, immediately reducing visibility to a few metres, imposing a remarkable leaden pall of silence and driving huge snowflakes into the eyes of anyone caught in the open. Yet such a blizzard might only last quarter of an hour, to be followed by crystal clear skies and a temperature which plummeted well below zero. Sheets of black ice then suddenly replaced the mud and slush, making walking virtually impossible.

Despite the possibility of such variable weather, the *knezes* Alexandre and Andrey led their men across the Velikaya river which flowed into the southern end of Lake Peipus, bypassed the Crusader garrison at Izborsk and swept into Bishop Hermann and the Teutonic Knights' lands south of Tartu. Here the countryside was similar to that around Pskov, being much more fertile than the Novgorod area. Today it is a mixture of deciduous forests and fields of barley or rye. Much the same would have been the case in the 13th century, though the fields would have been fewer and the forests more extensive. Scattered farmsteads still have deep sunken shed-like structures roofed with earth, presumably to store vegetables and other food supplies during the long winters. Freshwater fish from the many lakes and rivers are still smoked and cured for winter storage, as they would have been during the Middle Ages.

Although the numbers of troops involved in all these northern campaigns was small, even by medieval standards, the army led by Alexandre and Andrey was larger than those seen in 1240 and 1241. It is possible that the bulk of the professional troops on the Russian side were those sent by Yaroslav Vsevolodovich under Andrey's command. As such they may have been from the elite and substantial *druzhina* forces of central and southern Russia. They may also have included mounted archers of Turkish or even Mongol origin. Meanwhile Alexandre Nevskii's own *druzhina* was, according to the *Life of Alexandre Nevskii*, composed of men with *"hearts like lions' hearts"*.

Unlike the bronze doors of Novgorod Cathedral, those in Suzdal, in central Russia, were made by Russian craftsmen in the 13th century. Despite the strong Byzantine artistic influence on the archangel's armour to the left, the kneeling prince has an ordinary short-sleeved mail hauberk, European style mail chausses on his legs and a large kite-shaped shield. (*in situ* Rozhdestvensky Monastery, Suzdal, Russia)

Apparently relying on previous experience of Crusader lethargy, and at first meeting no resistance, Russian units spread across the countryside between Crusader-held Izborsk, Lake Peipus, the Crusader castle of Otepää and the fortified town of Tartu, causing as much damage as possible. Vengeance was their aim, as the *Livonian Rhymed Chronicle* made clear: "*But this* [Alexandre's retaking of Pskov] *was not the end of the matter. There is a great and powerful city, also in Russia, named Suzdal, and Alexandre was its king at that time* [actually it was his brother Andrey]. *He prepared his people for war and, because the Russians were grieved by their defeats, they were soon ready. Then king Alexandre, together with many other Russians, marched out from Suzdal. There were bowmen without number among them and many marvellous cuirasses. Their banners were splendid and their helmets bright for all to see. They advanced violently into the Order's lands* [Livonia] *with their army. Quickly the Brothers* [Teutonic Knights] *formed to oppose them, but there were very few of them. It was known in Dorpat* [Tartu] *that king Alexandre had come with an army into the Order's land to rob and burn. The Bishop* [Hermann of Tartu] *did not sit still, but ordered his men to hurry to the Brother's army and oppose the Russians. His command was obeyed, and in short order they joined the Brothers' forces. But they had brought along too few people, and the Brothers' army was also too small.*"

Nevertheless, the hurriedly assembled Crusader defenders soon scored a notable victory. The story, as seen from the Russian side, is continued by the *Chronicle of Novgorod*: "*...and* [Alexandre] *himself went against the Chud people* [Estonians]. *And when he came to their land, he let loose his whole force to provide for themselves. And Domash Tverdislavich and Kerbet were scouring the country and the Nemtsy and the Chud men met them by a bridge. And they fought there, and there they killed Domash, brother of the posadnik, an honest man, and others with him and others again they captured, and others escaped to the troops of the knez. And the knez turned back to the lake and the Nemtsy and the Chud men went after them.*"

This defeat of part of Alexandre's army is believed to have taken place at Mooste, south-east of Tartu, where the road from Pskov crosses a small stream and marsh. The name Mooste itself comes from the common Slav word for 'bridge' and in 13th century Estonia as in so much of medieval eastern Europe, the existence of any bridge was enough for it to give its name to a nearby settlement. In purely military terms, the bridge would also have created a choke-point where raiders could be ambushed. If this happened to the troops led by Domash Tverdislavich, it suggests that the spring thaw had already set in.

At Mooste a small stream now runs across fertile land which has been drained since the Middle Ages. It then flows through a small

Dense reed beds surround most of Lake Peipus on both the Estonian and Russian shores. They are occasionally pierced by paths down to the water's edge, as seen here from the landward side. (Author's photograph)

marsh, probably all that remains of a larger medieval swamp, and a small lake which may be the decorative man-made fishpond for the aristocratic manor which still exists. On the far side of this lake a modern road, probably following the same line as its medieval ancestor, crosses another marshy area via a long low bridge. The troops who ambushed Domash Tverdislavich and the ill-trained Novgorod militia whom he led seem to have been elite Teutonic Knights, almost certainly supported by Estonian auxiliaries who would have known the terrain in detail.

The survivors of this setback rejoined Alexandre Nevskii and the main Russian force. Alexandre's scouts would presumably have informed him that Bishop Hermann had also gathered his vassals and auxiliaries from Tartu and the rest of Ungannia. These formed the bulk of an army now marching against the Russians. Whether Alexandre Nevskii realised that the Bishop had been joined by many of the Danish King's vassals from Wierland in northern Estonia, and perhaps also Teutonic Knights' vassals from Jerwen province, north of Ungannia, remains doubtful. The *Livonian Rhymed Chronicle* makes much of the fact that the defending Crusaders were greatly outnumbered by the Russian invaders. But at the same time it specifies that "*the King's men*" – namely Danish vassals from Wierland – were present, so the Crusader army was a respectable force. The Teutonic Knights were represented in small numbers but they were a dedicated and superbly equipped fighting elite, so that the Crusaders' numerical inferiority should have been offset by their training, discipline and heavier weaponry.

Most Teutonic Knights based in this part of Livonia would have been ex-Sword Brethren. Their leadership is unknown, though it might have included Rudolf Von Kassel, the castellan of Wenden to the south-west of Tartu. Alexandre either felt that he had punished the Crusaders enough or was deterred from attacking Tartu itself because, according to a slightly later reference in the *Novgorod Chronicle,* it was defended by "three walls". Or he considered that the approaching Crusader army was too powerful. Whatever his motives, he turned eastward and headed towards Novgorodian territory – across the frozen surface of Lake Peipus.

One of the many beaches around Lake Peipus. This is at Meerapalu on the Estonian shore, at roughly the point from where the Crusader army is believed to have set out across the ice in pursuit of Alexandre Nevskii. (Author's photograph)

PRELUDE TO BATTLE OF LAKE PEIPUS
MARCH–5TH APRIL 1242

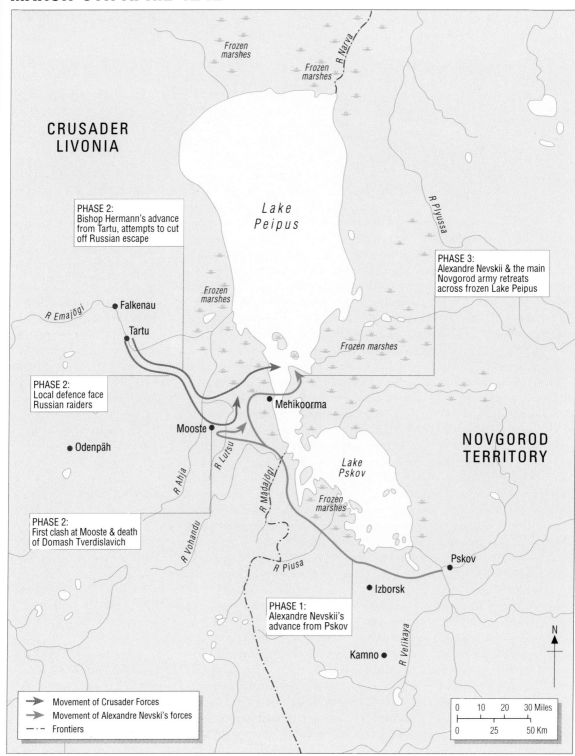

Frozen marshes

Frozen marshes

R Narva

CRUSADER LIVONIA

Lake Peipus

R Pivussa

PHASE 2:
Bishop Hermann's advance from Tartu, attempts to cut off Russian escape

PHASE 3:
Alexandre Nevskii & the main Novgorod army retreats across frozen Lake Peipus

Frozen marshes

R Emajõgi

● Falkenau

Tartu

Frozen marshes

PHASE 2:
Local defence face Russian raiders

● Mehikoorma

Mooste ●

NOVGOROD TERRITORY

● Odenpäh

R Ahja

R Luťsu

Lake Pskov

R Mädajõgi

Frozen marshes

PHASE 2:
First clash at Mooste & death of Domash Tverdislavich

R Vohandu

R Piusa

Pskov ●

● Izborsk

PHASE 1:
Alexandre Nevskii's advance from Pskov

R Velikaya

N

Kamno ●

→	Movement of Crusader Forces
→	Movement of Alexandre Nevski's forces
–·–·	Frontiers

| 0 | 10 | 20 | 30 Miles |

| 0 | 25 | | 50 Km |

THE BATTLE OF
LAKE PEIPUS

One aspect of this campaign which has caught the popular imagination is the fact that it was fought, at least in part, on the surface of a frozen lake. Yet this has itself led to widespread misunderstanding – strongly reinforced by Eisenstein's brilliant film, *Alexandre Nevskii*.

The shoreline of Lake Peipus is very flat and from spring to autumn substantial waves often break upon the beach as a result of strong prevailing winds and the low-lying character of the area. The shoreline itself consists of alternating beaches covered with small freshwater mussel shells and extensive reed banks which spread far out into the lake. According to Estonian border guards, the narrowest part of the hourglass-shaped lake is no more than one and a half to two metres deep. These narrows divide the largest stretch of water (Lake Peipus itself) in the north from the smaller stretch (often known as Lake Pskov) to the south. In fact these narrows consist of two straits enclosing a small third piece of water (sometimes called Lake Lammi). Furthermore the southernmost arm of Lake Peipus is separated from the rest of the lake by the large Piirissaar island. This means that there are three narrows where the lake as a whole could be crossed, and their strategic importance was again demonstrated when the Red Army made a successful amphibious crossing in 1944.

The area where the Crusaders are believed to have crossed the lake is particularly low-lying, windswept and prone to flooding. In fact its shores consist of dense reed-beds which also extend far inland. Sand-bars can reduce the water-depth at the mouths of the several small rivers to only 30 centimetres. In complete contrast, the Estonian island of Piirissaar, lying midway between the Estonian and Russian shores, is remarkably fertile, though still surrounded by reed-beds.

Unlike the Russian crossing during the Second World War, both Alexandre Nevskii and his Crusader foes crossed when the lake was frozen. This did not, however, mean that they rode across a smooth sheet of ice. According to local information, the ice on Lake Peipus does not all lie flat in winter. Instead it is often piled into small jagged pinnacles and overlapping planks by the prevailing wind as it freezes, partially melts, then freezes again in late autumn. This is mostly seen on the lee shore which, given the prevailing winter wind from the west, would be down the eastern side of the lake and its various off-shore islands. Furthermore the ice tends to melt first around its edges in spring, though in early March this ice would normally still be from 20 to 50 centimetres thick; quite enough to support infantry and dispersed cavalry, though dangerous for heavily armoured horsemen in close formation.

Unfortunately the precise route taken by the two armies is not

known. The original sources only mention where they started, and where the final battle is believed to have taken place – though even this is a matter of conjecture. Since frozen marshes and rivers traditionally formed the main routes in Russian and Baltic winter warfare, Alexandre can be assumed to have headed for what is now the fishing village of Mehikoorma on the Estonian side of the main 'narrows', this being his

LEFT **Dozens of little carvings on the outside of Vladimir Cathedral, 1193-1197, include a few armed figures such as these huntsmen and fabulous beasts. Most of their military equipment, as well as horse harness and clothing, is more western European than Byzantine or oriental in style, indicating that early medieval Russia was not so different from the rest of Europe. (in situ Cathedral of Dimitri Sobor, Vladimir, Russia)**

most obvious route back to friendly territory. The movement of Bishop Hermann's Crusader force is more doubtful. If he and his Teutonic Knight comrades were bent on catching the Russians, as the sources suggest, and if he had good information from his local Estonian scouts, he might have turned abruptly east. This would have taken him over frozen marshland to cross the lake slightly further north, where he could hopefully cut Alexandre off near the modern Russian fishing village of Samolva. Alternatively, he might have crossed via Piirissaar island, though this would have been a longer journey.

It would seem that Alexandre Nevskii's scouts kept him well informed, for instead of heading directly towards Novgorod he turned north as soon as his army reached the Russian side of the lake, heading for a place called the Raven's Rock. The author was unable to identify this precise spot despite the fact that there are very few such rocky outcrops along the shores of Lake Peipus. It is, however, generally considered by both Russian and Estonian historians to have been at the northern tip of a flat peninsula jutting towards Piirissaar island. Alexandre's precise motives remain unknown, but the lie of the land, or rather of the shoreline and its series of tiny off-shore islets, when added to his decision to face the Crusaders in open battle, makes tactical sense of Alexandre's move. It would have made even more sense if jagged ice-floes had indeed built up along the lee shore, since these could have provided a ready-made field fortification.

All that the *Novgorod Chronicle* says is: "*Seeing this* [that the Crusaders were following him], *knez Alexandre and all the men of Novgorod drew up their forces on Lake Chud* [Lake Peipus] *at Uzmen* [unknown] *by the Voroni Kamen* [Raven's Rock]." In reality the Russians are unlikely to have formed ranks on the frozen surface of the lake, but rather on the beach and land immediately behind, with any jumbled ice-floes ahead of them.

The subsequent battle is presented in the *Life of Alexandre Nevskii* in a purely traditional and rather unhelpful manner. Both sides meet on the lake, the pious Prince Alexandre prays and then the armies clash: "*It was Saturday, at sunrise, that the two armies met, and there was terrible carnage, and the crash of spears and their breaking and the clash of swords smiting as they moved over the frozen sea, and you could not see the ice, it was covered with blood.*" Nevertheless, the *Life of Alexandre Nevskii* does make the interesting assertion that the Crusaders' primary aim was to kill or capture Alexandre Nevskii himself; a normal tactic under the circumstances. In response the strong and brave members of Alexandre's *druzhina* declare: "*O our honourable knez, now is the time for us to sacrifice our heads for you.*"

The other sources are more helpful, but provide only a few tantalising details. The most important is that the Crusaders attacked in a wedge formation which was, of course, normal for a *cuneus*, or unit of armoured knights, and that some of the fighting took place on the ice itself. According to the *Novgorod Chronicle*: "*An army of Nemtsy and Chuds came upon them, and they fought their way through his army in a wedge. And there was a great battle with the Nemtsys and Chuds, with the crash of shattering spears and the sound of clashing swords, so that even the frozen sea moved and the ice could not be seen, for all was covered with blood.*"

From the opposing camp the *Livonian Rhymed Chronicle* stated: "*Nevertheless they* [the outnumbered Crusaders] *decided to attack the Russians. The latter had many archers, and the battle began with their bold*

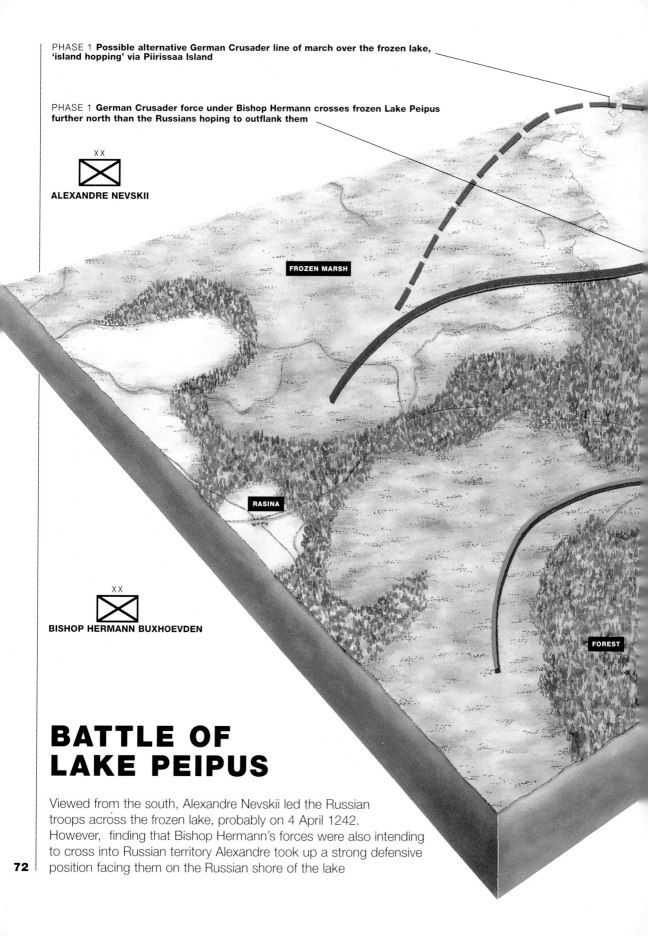

PHASE 1 **Possible alternative German Crusader line of march over the frozen lake, 'island hopping' via Piirissaa Island**

PHASE 1 **German Crusader force under Bishop Hermann crosses frozen Lake Peipus further north than the Russians hoping to outflank them**

X X

ALEXANDRE NEVSKII

FROZEN MARSH

RASINA

X X

BISHOP HERMANN BUXHOEVDEN

FOREST

BATTLE OF LAKE PEIPUS

Viewed from the south, Alexandre Nevskii led the Russian troops across the frozen lake, probably on 4 April 1242. However, finding that Bishop Hermann's forces were also intending to cross into Russian territory Alexandre took up a strong defensive position facing them on the Russian shore of the lake

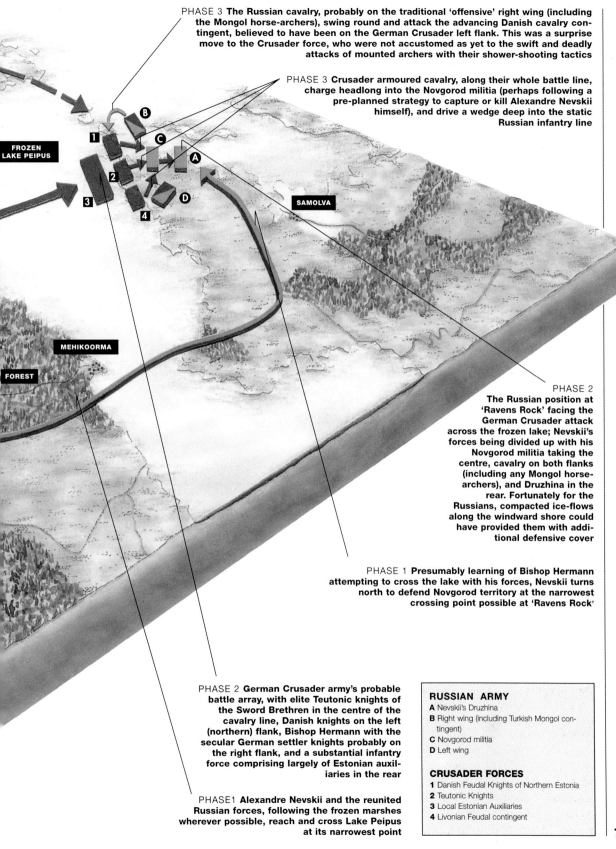

PHASE 3 The Russian cavalry, probably on the traditional 'offensive' right wing (including the Mongol horse-archers), swing round and attack the advancing Danish cavalry contingent, believed to have been on the German Crusader left flank. This was a surprise move to the Crusader force, who were not accustomed as yet to the swift and deadly attacks of mounted archers with their shower-shooting tactics

PHASE 3 Crusader armoured cavalry, along their whole battle line, charge headlong into the Novgorod militia (perhaps following a pre-planned strategy to capture or kill Alexandre Nevskii himself), and drive a wedge deep into the static Russian infantry line

FROZEN LAKE PEIPUS

B

1

C

A

2

3

D

4

SAMOLVA

MEHIKOORMA

FOREST

PHASE 2
The Russian position at 'Ravens Rock' facing the German Crusader attack across the frozen lake; Nevskii's forces being divided up with his Novgorod militia taking the centre, cavalry on both flanks (including any Mongol horse-archers), and Druzhina in the rear. Fortunately for the Russians, compacted ice-flows along the windward shore could have provided them with additional defensive cover

PHASE 1 Presumably learning of Bishop Hermann attempting to cross the lake with his forces, Nevskii turns north to defend Novgorod territory at the narrowest crossing point possible at 'Ravens Rock'

PHASE 2 German Crusader army's probable battle array, with elite Teutonic knights of the Sword Brethren in the centre of the cavalry line, Danish knights on the left (northern) flank, Bishop Hermann with the secular German settler knights probably on the right flank, and a substantial infantry force comprising largely of Estonian auxiliaries in the rear

PHASE1 Alexandre Nevskii and the reunited Russian forces, following the frozen marshes wherever possible, reach and cross Lake Peipus at its narrowest point

RUSSIAN ARMY
A Nevskii's Druzhina
B Right wing (including Turkish Mongol contingent)
C Novgorod militia
D Left wing

CRUSADER FORCES
1 Danish Feudal Knights of Northern Estonia
2 Teutonic Knights
3 Local Estonian Auxiliaries
4 Livonian Feudal contingent

assault on the King's men [vassals of the Danish crown from northern Estonia]. *The Brothers'* [Teutonic Knights'] *banners were soon flying in the midst of the archers, and the swords were heard cutting helmets apart. Many from both sides fell dead on the grass."*

Though sparse, this information is enough, when added to the known military traditions of both sides, to make a tentative reconstruction of each army's battle array. The *Livonian Rhymed Chronicle* does not differentiate between the bulk of the Russian infantry archers, who would normally have been at the centre of a traditional Russian array, and the smaller number of mounted archers of presumed Turkish or Mongol origin who would, according to their military traditions, have been on one or both flanks. If these horse-archers were Kipchaqs or other such Turkish refugees, their tactics would already have been strongly influenced by Middle Eastern Islamic and Byzantine practice, in which case they could be expected to have been stationed on the traditionally offensive right flank of the Russian battle-line – the northern end of Alexandre's array.

The Russians themselves had, of course, also been under strong Byzantine and Iranian military influence for centuries. The 'offensive' rather than 'defensive' archers attacked the King's men, namely the Danish vassals, but the location of the latter is not specified. Yet there are two reasons why they might also have been on the northern edge of the battlefield. The Teutonic Knights' contingent, as a recognised military elite, is likely to have been at the centre or on the more prestigious right (southern) wing. Bishop Hermann's own militia is also likely to have been in the centre, since he probably commanded the army. This leaves the King's men with the less prestigious left (northern) wing. Such an array would also have mirrored the geographical origins of the various contingents, with the Danish vassals in the north, Bishop Hermann's militia and the Military Order in the centre or the south. The more lightly armed local Estonian auxiliaries would have brought up the rear.

The battle itself was brief but hard fought. Most of it probably took place on the beach rather than the frozen lake, as the Crusader

When seen from the lake itself, the shores of Lake Peipus generally present an impenetrable wall of reeds, though the water is extremely shallow. This is the shoreline of Piirissaar island. (Author's photograph)

armoured cavalry drove deep into the static Russian line. But the issue had perhaps already been decided on the northern flank, where Alexandre's allied Turkish or Mongol horse-archers routed or at least disrupted the Danish vassals. Even the reference to divine *"aerial"* intervention mentioned by a supposed eye-witness in the *Life of Alexandre Nevskii* probably reflected the action of these horse-archers. Their shower-shooting tactics would as yet have been unknown to the Crusaders. They may still have been a novelty to the Russian author, whose description of God's Host coming through the air to help Alexandre could be an echo of the whistling rain of arrows which fell upon the surprised King's men.

Once they hit the Russian line, the Crusader knights soon found themselves surrounded, as bitter fighting developed on both flanks. Not only was Alexandre's army larger than that of Bishop Hermann, but the latter's Estonian auxiliaries soon fled – if indeed they did ever come into contact with the enemy. Once these local troops had either hesitated or withdrawn, the German and Danish knights and sergeants would have been hugely outnumbered. As the *Life of Alexandre Nevskii* stated: *"With God's help he vanquished them, and the enemy forces turned and fled. But they [Alexandre's army] smote and pursued as if from the air; there was no place to which they [the Crusaders] could flee."*

The *Livonian Rhymed Chronicle* admitted the totality of Crusader defeat: *"Then the Brothers' army was completely surrounded, for the Russians had so many troops that there were easily sixty men for every one German knight."*

The *Novgorod Chronicle* also attributed victory to divine aid: *"And there was great slaughter of Nemtsy and Chud men. And God and St. Sophia and the Holy Martyrs Boris and Gleb, for whose sake the men of Novgorod shed their blood, by the great prayers of those Saints, God helped knez Alexandre."*

David stops his men from killing King Saul, in the Russian Simonov-Chludov Psalter of c.1270. (Location unknown)

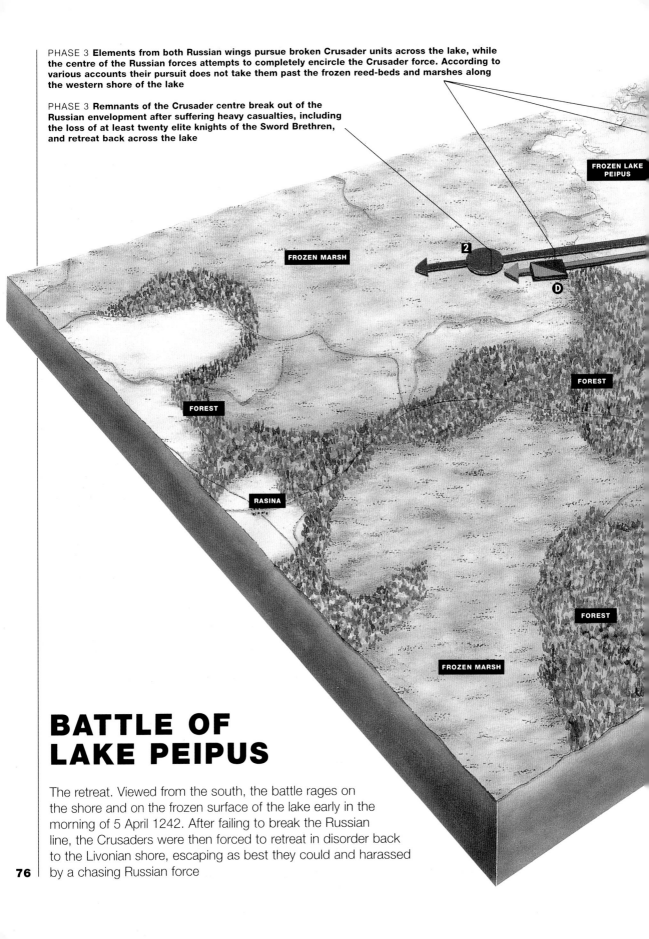

PHASE 3 **Elements from both Russian wings pursue broken Crusader units across the lake, while the centre of the Russian forces attempts to completely encircle the Crusader force. According to various accounts their pursuit does not take them past the frozen reed-beds and marshes along the western shore of the lake**

PHASE 3 **Remnants of the Crusader centre break out of the Russian envelopment after suffering heavy casualties, including the loss of at least twenty elite knights of the Sword Brethren, and retreat back across the lake**

FROZEN LAKE PEIPUS

FROZEN MARSH

2

D

FOREST

FOREST

RASINA

FOREST

FROZEN MARSH

BATTLE OF LAKE PEIPUS

The retreat. Viewed from the south, the battle rages on the shore and on the frozen surface of the lake early in the morning of 5 April 1242. After failing to break the Russian line, the Crusaders were then forced to retreat in disorder back to the Livonian shore, escaping as best they could and harassed by a chasing Russian force

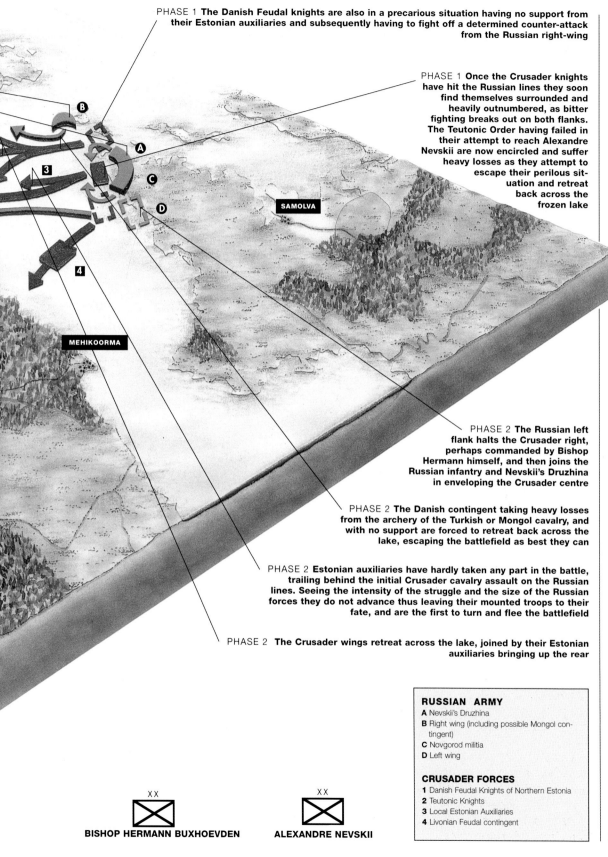

PHASE 1 **The Danish Feudal knights are also in a precarious situation having no support from their Estonian auxiliaries and subsequently having to fight off a determined counter-attack from the Russian right-wing**

PHASE 1 **Once the Crusader knights have hit the Russian lines they soon find themselves surrounded and heavily outnumbered, as bitter fighting breaks out on both flanks. The Teutonic Order having failed in their attempt to reach Alexandre Nevskii are now encircled and suffer heavy losses as they attempt to escape their perilous situation and retreat back across the frozen lake**

SAMOLVA

MEHIKOORMA

PHASE 2 **The Russian left flank halts the Crusader right, perhaps commanded by Bishop Hermann himself, and then joins the Russian infantry and Nevskii's Druzhina in enveloping the Crusader centre**

PHASE 2 **The Danish contingent taking heavy losses from the archery of the Turkish or Mongol cavalry, and with no support are forced to retreat back across the lake, escaping the battlefield as best they can**

PHASE 2 **Estonian auxiliaries have hardly taken any part in the battle, trailing behind the initial Crusader cavalry assault on the Russian lines. Seeing the intensity of the struggle and the size of the Russian forces they do not advance thus leaving their mounted troops to their fate, and are the first to turn and flee the battlefield**

PHASE 2 **The Crusader wings retreat across the lake, joined by their Estonian auxiliaries bringing up the rear**

X X
BISHOP HERMANN BUXHOEVDEN

X X
ALEXANDRE NEVSKII

RUSSIAN ARMY
A Nevskii's Druzhina
B Right wing (including possible Mongol contingent)
C Novgorod militia
D Left wing

CRUSADER FORCES
1 Danish Feudal Knights of Northern Estonia
2 Teutonic Knights
3 Local Estonian Auxiliaries
4 Livonian Feudal contingent

The retreat of the Estonian auxiliaries is emphasised in both Livonian and Russian sources, though they were clearly not the only ones to escape. According to the *Novgorod Chronicle*: "*The Nemtsy fell there, and the Chuds took flight. They were pursued and slain on the ice for seven versts* [about 7.5 kilometres] *to the Sobolitskii* [western] *shore. And countless Chuds fells, and four hundred Nemtsy, and fifty others were taken prisoner and brought to Novgorod. And they fought on April 5th, on a Saturday, the Commemoration day of the holy Martyr Feodor, to the Glory of the Holy Mother of God.*"

The figure of "*seven versts*" must be treated with caution. But it is interesting to note that it is approximately the distance from the presumed location of the battle to the Estonian side of the lake. Perhaps this confirms the site of the battle and indicates that the pursuing Russians did not venture far into the frozen reed-beds and marshes along the western shore. According to the *Livonian Rhymed Chronicle*: "*The Brothers* [Teutonic Knights] *fought well enough, but they were nevertheless cut down. Some of those from Dorpat* [the Estonian auxiliaries of Bishop Hermann of Tartu] *escaped from the battle, and it was their salvation that they had been forced to flee. Twenty Brothers lay dead and six were captured.*"

Even the casualty figures in German and Russian sources tally, up to a point. The *Novgorod Chronicle*'s claim of 400 German and Danish dead, though almost certainly exaggerated, would have included the 20 elite Teutonic Knights admitted by the *Livonian Rhymed Chronicle*, while the

When the spring thaw sets in, the ice of Russia's northern lakes does not flow regularly downstream. One day there will be virtually no ice whilst the next day, the river can be virtually choked with ice-floes, as seen here on the river Neva in the heart of Saint Petersburg in March. (Author's photograph)

latter's claim of 50 enemy captured would have included other soldiers in addition to the six Teutonic Knights mentioned in the *Rhymed Chronicle*. Furthermore, it has been suggested, on the basis of his disappearance from future records, that the troublesome ex-Sword Brother Rudolf Von Kassel was one of those slain.

The campaign ended with Alexandre's return home. Not surprisingly, the *Livonian Rhymed Chronicle* regretted the outcome but preferred to move on to other matters: *"Thus the battle ended. King Alexandre was happy that he had won the battle, and he returned home. But he paid for his victory, for he left behind many a bold man who would never again ride to war. As for the Brothers who were slain in the battle, they were later mourned, along with many other undaunted heroes. Many of those who, in God's Name, took up the life of the Teutonic Order have, from those days to these, been slain in the service of God. Also, at other times, they subdued the lands with a mailed fist, as I shall now relate. But this episode is now ended."*

The *Life of Alexandre Nevskii* was, of course, triumphal in tone, describing how Alexandre was met by the people, abbots and priests of Pskov. They came out carrying crosses to greet him and to praise God – perhaps also to ensure that their city was not punished for its previous welcoming of the Germans. Alexandre then proceeded to Novgorod, leading captive *"those who are called knights"* tied to the harness of their own and other captured war-horses. As the *Novgorod Chronicle* continued: *"The name of Alexandre became famed in all the lands . . . as far as Rome itself."*

Both sides were now, for differing reasons, eager to make peace. According to the *Novgorod Chronicle*: *"The same year the Nemtsy sent greeting, in the absence of the knez* [Alexandre having apparently already left Novgorod to deal with the greater problem of relations with the Mongols], *saying, 'The land of the Vod people, of Luga, Pskov and Lotygola, which we invaded with the sword, from all this we withdraw, and those of your men whom we have taken we will exchange, we will let go yours and you let go ours.' And they let go the Pskov hostages, and made peace."*

Sleeping guards at the Holy Sepulchre on a painted north German wood carving of 1250-1300. The figure on the right wears a coat-of-plates and has his great helm on his knee. (Provincial Museum, Hannover, Germany)

AFTERMATH AND RECKONING

CONSEQUENCES FOR THE CRUSADERS

The Crusade against Novgorod failed because the papal legate, William of Modena, could not muster enough men for the task. Like all those involved, he did not appreciate the degree to which Russian states would co-operate in a crisis and he clearly underestimated the military potential of Russia as a whole. The Crusaders' defeat in the battle of Lake Peipus was also a result of supreme overconfidence, along with the fact that Alexandre Nevskii's army included a sufficiently large number of horse-archers to disrupt the Crusader attack. The presence of these archers was also not expected by the Crusaders.

RIGHT **The seal of the German city of Bamberg showing Saint Maurice in reverse, since this is the seal itself rather than the impression it makes. Though the knight has an old fashioned pointed helmet, the dots around his shoulders might indicate a modern coat-of-plates. (inv. nr. 13/24, Historisches Museum, Bamberg, Germany)**

The peace negotiations which followed meant that the Crusaders handed back all the lands they had conquered, including the castle of Izborsk. But it did not bring peace to the Crusader territories themselves. Native Baltic revolts broke out almost at once in Kurland and Prussia, and shortly afterwards in Estonia. The most serious was to the south, where the Prussian elders had already made contact with the Christian Slav Duke Sventopolk of Pomerallia (now the Polish coastal region west of Gdansk) following the Mongol victory at Liegnitz in 1241. The resulting widespread uprising against Teutonic Knights' rule lasted seven years.

The defeat of the Novgorod Crusade similarly led to a new relationship between Catholics and Orthodox in the Baltic, with a new Pope, Innocent IV, trying to win over the Russians diplomatically rather than by military means. More than half the Brothers killed at Lake Peipus were probably ex-Sword Brethren, and this finally broke the old Order's influence within the Teutonic

NEVSKII'S HORSE ARCHERS ATTACK THE DANISH FLANK

The identity of those archers who played such a decisive role in the battle of Lake Peipus remains uncertain. They were, however, almost certainly horse-archers on the right flank of Alexandre's army. As such they are likely to have been allied Kipchaq Turks or newly arrived representatives of Russia's Mongol conquerors. Their victims were the unsuspecting 'King's Men', vassals of the Danish crown, on the left wing of the Crusader army.

Statue of Count Eckhart, one of the founders of Naumberg Cathedral, mid 13th century. (*in situ* Cathedral, Naumberg, Germany)

Knights. The battle had also convinced a chastened Bishop Hermann of Tartu to accept the Teutonic Knights' priorities, which were to crush the pagan Lithuanians and to Christianise all the Baltic lands, rather than interfering in Russian affairs.

Finally, these events gave the Landmeister Dietrich Von Grüningen a chance to reform and restructure the Teutonic Knights in Livonia; a task he carried out so efficiently that he was elected Master of Prussia in 1246 and then Grand Master in 1254. The final version of the *Statutes of the Order of Teutonic Knights* was also drawn up in the aftermath of the Novgorod Crusade. This imposed much greater discipline and insisted that only noble recruits would be accepted – unlike the old Sword Brethren, who had accepted recruits of lower social status. Teutonic Knights' belligerence remained unchanged, however, and soon led to criticism within some parts of the Church. As Roger Bacon, an English friar, wrote some years later: *"The Prussians would have been converted long ago if it was not for the violence of the Teutonic Order, because the pagan people have many times been prepared to receive the Faith in peace following preaching. But those of the Teutonic House do not wish to allow this, because they wish to subjugate them and reduce them to slavery, and by subtle persuasions they have already for many years deceived the Roman Church."*

The collapse of the Novgorod Crusade also had its effect in Danish-ruled northern Estonia and even in neighbouring Finland. Within Estonia the new Danish king, Eric IV, gave greater autonomy to the Bishop of Tallinn, while real power remained in the hands of the leaders of local 'knightly corporations'. Nevertheless, Estonia remained a burden rather than a benefit for the Danes, who finally sold it to the Teutonic Knights in 1346. Further north, the Swedish threat to Novgorod lay dormant until the mid 14th century, while Bishop Thomas resigned in 1245, convinced that he had failed in his life's work of converting the Finns and Karelians. In fact this English-born bishop was over pessimistic. Earl Karl Birger rebounded from his defeat by Alexandre Nevskii on the river Neva to lead other Crusades, after which there was a massive Swedish colonisation of south-western Finland.

Part of a copy of a very damaged and now lost wall painting made in 1227, showing German knights jousting. (*in situ* Wartburg Castle, Eisenach, Germany)

CONSEQUENCES FOR THE RUSSIANS

Alexandre Nevskii had defeated the Crusader invasion by swift action and by assembling adequate forces, most notably by having a force of Turkish or Mongol horse-archers in his army at the battle of Lake Peipus. The rest of his career shows him to have been an effective military commander and an even more skilled politician. Following his victory in 1242, Alexandre did not invade Crusader territory. He knew that the Teutonic Knights remained strong, though at that moment overstretched, and that many large Crusader garrisons stood along the Baltic coast. But above all Alexandre Nevskii was more concerned about the Mongols. Consequently he offered generous terms, which the Crusaders immediately accepted, resulting in 20 years of relative peace except for a Russian raid against the Emi tribesmen of southern Finland in 1256.

For Novgorod itself, the events of 1240–1242 proved that the city was unable to resist Crusader encroachment on its own, and so the necessity of rule by a *knez* or prince was grudgingly accepted. In fact, under Alexandre, Novgorod consolidated its hold over the Arctic north and as far east as the Ural mountains.

Peace with the Crusaders did not, however, mean peace along all of Russia's north-western frontier. The rising power of still-pagan Lithuania developed into a major menace despite Alexandre Nevskii's own success in defeating three large-scale Lithuanian raids.

In reality Alexandre's victories over the Swedes on the river Neva and the largely German Crusaders on Lake Peipus were relatively minor affairs of only local significance. The *Hypatius Chronicle* from southern Russia, for example, stated that *"Nothing happened"* in both 1240 and 1242. But this did not stop later chroniclers, particularly the author of the *Life of Alexandre Nevskii*, blowing them into epic proportions – perhaps to compensate for the embarrassment of Alexandre Nevskii's close relations with the Mongol conquerors. The *Life of Alexandre Nevskii* goes out of its way to show the invading Catholic Crusaders as a great and wicked enemy, whereas it portrays the Mongols in a quite sympathetic light. Even the canonisation of Alexandre as an Orthodox Christian Saint in 1381 was part of an effort to promote the prestige of Moscow's ruling dynasty against its Russian rivals – this dynasty having been descended from Alexandre Nevskii himself.

Alexandre's relations with the Mongols were based upon pragmatism and unswerving loyalty to the Orthodox Church. He also realised that resistance to the 'world conquerors' would mean disaster. So he not only submitted, but collected taxes for them and visited the Mongol Golden Horde's capital on the river Volga several times. In the words of the *Novgorod Chronicle*: *"In the year 1246 the stern prince Alexandre went to the*

Effigy of the Count Von Gleichen and his two (successive) wives, mid 13th century. (*in situ* Cathedral, Erfurt, Germany)

RIGHT **The countryside and villages around Novgorod remain much as they were when Crusader raiders ravaged the area in the 13th century, despite Soviet collectivisation and more modern (though still primitive) wooden houses. This is Uspenskoye in early spring. (Author's photograph)**

RIGHT **The battle of Lake Peipus, as shown in a 16th century Russian manuscript. It was only then, when the story of Alexandre Nevskii's victory had reached epic proportions, that the idea of invading Crusaders falling through the ice entered the story. (Kremlin Museum, Novgorod, Russia)**

FLIGHT OF BISHOP HERMANN'S FORCES

Bishop Hermann of Tartu, commander of the Crusader force in 1242, escaped from the débâcle on Lake Peipus, as did the bulk of the Crusader army (the Bishop's own Estonian auxilaries were the first to flee). Alexandre's men pursued them at least as far as the Estonian shore of the lake, and probably slightly further. Since the bulk of the escaping Crusader force was mounted, it must have been the minority of horsemen in Alexandre's army which chased them. In this picture, Bishop Hermann's coat-of-arms is based on the earliest known seals of the city of Tartu.

Tartar land to the Tsar Batu. For the Tsar had spoken to him thus: 'God has subjugated all the nations to me; you alone do not wish to subjugate yourself to me, nor to my power. But if you wish to preserve your land, come to me and see the glory of my realm...' Prince Alexandre went straightway to Bishop Kiril and spoke these words to him: 'Father, I want to go to the Horde, to the Tsar.' Bishop Kiril, with all the clergy, blessed him and he went to the Tsar Batu . . . The Tsar Batu gave great honour and gifts to the Russian Prince Alexandre and dismissed him with great affection."

It was, in fact, because of Alexandre's loyalty that the Mongols let him become *Veliki Knez* in 1252, following the crushing of a revolt by the previous *Veliki Knez*, Alexandre's less astute brother Andrey. Ordinary people still sometimes resisted Mongol tax collectors, and it was on his way home from pleading mercy for the people of Novgorod, who had driven out the Mongols' tax assessors, that Alexandre Nevskii died. Feeling the approach of his death, Alexandre *"was shorn"* as a monk on 14 November 1263 and died the following night. He was buried in the Monastery of the Nativity at Vladimir.

Archbishop Kiril was finishing the Eucharist when news of Alexandre's death reached him, and turning to the congregation he said: *"The Sun of the Russian land has set, my children."*

The *Novgorod Chronicle* was equally generous, stating: *"Grant him, O Merciful Lord, to see Thy Face in the future age, for he laboured for Novgorod and for all the Russian land."*

THE BATTLEFIELDS TODAY

Like so many interesting battlefields, that of Lake Peipus lies on an international frontier. Travel within Estonia is, however, unrestricted, while in Russia, following the collapse of the Soviet Union, it has become much easier – at least in terms of closed or restricted areas. The precise location of the battle of the river Neva is disputed, though it certainly did not take place where St. Petersburg now stands, nor where Tsar Peter the Great erected his Alexandre Nevskii monastery. In fact it is likely to have been further up river, perhaps where the Neva exits from Lake Ladoga. These locations can most easily be reached from St. Petersburg by taxi or hire-car. (Hiring a taxi for the day remains the most efficient means of local travel in Russia.)

Novgorod and Pskov are major historical, cultural and tourist centres with adequate hotels. Public transport between these and St. Petersburg is almost ridiculously cheap, while at the same time frequent. The dramatic fortress of Izborsk is about an hour's drive from Pskov. Unfortunately the territory further west, around Petseri, is still technically disputed between Russia and Estonia, with the former in control. The main road and rail link between St. Petersburg and the Estonian

RIGHT **Pskov's citadel or kremlin, seen from the north. The massive fortifications which now dominate the site largely date from the 15th century.**

Tower 4 of Novgorod's later medieval fortifications, seen from tower 3 and with the river Volkhov in the background. (Author's photograph)

capital of Tallinn runs to the south of the castle of Koporye. This coastal region is still rather sensitive, being virtually all that remains of Russia's Baltic coast. Nevertheless, with sufficient checking beforehand, Koporye can be reached from St. Petersburg or Sosnovyy Bor.

The Russian side of Lake Peipus, where the main battle took place, again remains a sensitive frontier area, though it can be visited either on the off-chance that the local police are feeling relaxed or after making the arrangements in Pskov. Once again a taxi for the day seems the best option. The nearest one can normally get to the presumed site of the

The existing fortifications of Izborsk largely date from the 14th century. It is still unclear whether the castle captured by the Crusaders was here or at Truvor's farmstead outside the town.

The Russian tsar Peter the Great demolished all stone structures in the medieval town of Tartu when he conquered Estonia. All that remains are a few fragments of the city wall which dates from the 13th century. (Author's photograph)

BELOW **Statue of an archangel carrying a large form of late 12th-early 13th century shield. Three dimensional representations of the interior of shields from this period are extremely rare. (*In situ* Cathedral, Bamberg, Germany)**

battle are, however, the villages of Samolva or Tsudskaja Rudnitsa. Both are within walking distance of the lake shore, though 4 kilometres of marshy reed beds and woods from the battlefield. Things are altogether easier on the Estonian side, with plenty of hotel accommodation. Peter the Great razed the stone structures of Tartu to the ground, including the medieval city wall. Nevertheless, this delightful university town remains the best centre from which to explore the campaign area, though Põlva has hotels as well as camp-sites. As in Russia, hiring a taxi for the day is the easiest means of transport and is relatively cheap, while self-drive cars can normally only be obtained in Tallinn.

The 19th century 'great house' at Mooste, which belonged to the baronial Von Nölken family until 1945, still stands, though its gardens are now in a sorry state. The fertile surrounding countryside is pretty rather than dramatic, and it takes an effort of imagination to conjure up the bleak primitive forests and marshes of the 13th century. Extensive marshes and reed beds do exist around Lake Peipus, and the south-western shores of the lake are still home to a Russian minority, including members of the Old Believers sect, which fled from Peter the Great's religious persecutions in the late 17th century. Unlike the Russian side of the lake, the Estonian shore is dotted with numerous villages. From the largest of these, Mehikoorma, a modern ferry sails to Piirissaar island, though a tiny fishing boat can also take those with stronger nerves across the windswept lake from the lakeside hamlet of Meerapalu.

CHRONOLOGY

1203 Kipchaq Turks ravage Kiev.

1204 Fourth Crusade conquers Byzantine capital of Constantinople.

1220 Birth of Alexandre Nevskii. Danes occupy northern Estonia and build Tallinn castle.

1223 First Mongol invasion of southern Russia: 16 June – Mongols defeat Russians and Kipchaqs at battle of Kalka river.

1224 Crusaders under Bishop Hermann conquer Estonian town of Tartu.

1227 January – Crusaders seize Ösel Island, ending first phase of Crusader conquest of Livonia. Danes defeated at Bornhöved; collapse of Danish Baltic Empire. Russian mission to convert pagan Karelians.

1228 Alexandre's first withdrawal from Novgorod.

1230 Pope gives Teutonic Knights authority to conquer pagan Prussians.

1236 Alexandre becomes *knez* of Novgorod. Beginning of Mongol invasion of Europe. Sword Brethren and Crusaders virtually annihilated by Lithuanians at battle of Saule.

1237-40 Second Mongol invasion of Russia.

1237 Allied Crusader and Russian army defeated by Lithuanians. Start of organisation of Novgorod Crusade.

1238 March – Mongol army turns back a few kilometres from Novgorod. Abolition of Sword Brethren, division of their lands between Teutonic Knights and Danes. Treaty of Stensby settles outstanding disputes between Danes, Teutonic Knights and Livonian Bishops.

1240-41 Winter – Crusaders invade Novgorodian territory north-east of Lake Peipus and seize Koporye.

1240 Swedes invade Novgorodian territory. 12 July – Alexandre defeats Swedes at battle of river Neva.

1241 9 April – Mongols defeat Poles and Germans at battle of Liegnitz. 12 April – Mongols defeat Hungarians at battle of Mohi. Autumn – Alexandre retakes Koporye and surrounding area; Crusaders seize Izborsk, south of Lake Peipus. 15 September Crusaders defeat army of Pskov and take Pskov.

1242 5 March – Alexandre retakes Pskov and raids Crusader territory. Start of April – local Crusader defence forces defeat part of Alexandre's army at Mooste. 5 April – Alexandre defeats Crusader army at Lake Peipus.

1242-49 Prussian uprising against Teutonic Knights.

1243 Estonian uprising against Danes.

1246 Alexandre officially submits to Mongol Khan Batu.

1252 Alexandre becomes *Veliki Knez* (Grand Prince) of Russia under Mongol overlordship.

1263 Death of Alexandre Nevskii.

FURTHER READING

Benninghoven, F., *Der Orden der Schwertbrüder* (Cologne-Graz 1965).

Brundage, J.A. (trans.), *The Chronicle of Henry of Livonia* (Madison 1961); covers the period before the Novgorod Crusade.

Brundage, J.A., 'The Thirteenth-Century Livonian Crusades', *Jahrbücher für Geschichte Osteuropas,* n.s. XX (1972), 1-9.

Christiansen, E., *The Northern Crusades: The Baltic and Catholic Frontier 1100-1525* (London 1980).

Dimnik, M., *Mikhail, Prince of Chernigov and Grand Prince of Kiev 1224-1246* (Toronto 1981).

Fennell, J., *The Crisis of Medieval Russia 1200-1304* (London 1983).

Fennell, J., *Early Russian Literature* (London 1974).

Gorelik, M.V., 'Bronya Praotecheskaya' (Ancient Armour), *Vokrug Sveta* (Moscow, May 1975), 64-65, in Russian.

Grégoire, H., R. Jakobson & M. Szeftet (trans. & edits.), 'La Geste du Prince Igor', *Annuaire de l'Institut de Philologie et d'Histoire Orientales et Slaves*, VIII (1945-47).

Gudzy, N.K. (trans. S. Wilbur-Jones), *History of Early Russian Literature* (New York 1949).

Hajdu, P. (trans. G.F. Cushing), *Finno-Ugrian Languages and Peoples* (London 1975).

Halperin, C.J., *Russia and the Golden Horde* (London 1985).

Johnson, E., 'The German Crusade in the Baltic', in H. Hazard (edit.), *A History of the Crusades, vol. III* (Madison 1975), 545-585.

Kirpitchnikoff, A., *Drevnerusskoe Oruzhie (Les Armes de la Russie Medievale)* (Leningrad 1971), in Russian with French summary.

Kirpitchnikoff, A., *Snapyazhenie Vsadnika i Verkhobogo Konya na Rusi IX-XIIIvv (Harnachement du Cavalier et de la Monture en Russie aux IX-XIII Siècles)* (Leningrad 1973), in Russian with French summary.

Kirpitchnikoff, A., *Voennoe Delo na Rusi v XIII-XV vv (L'Art Militarie en Russie des XIII-XV Siècles)* (Leningrad 1976), in Russian with French summary.

Kirpicnikov (Kirpitchnikoff), A., 'Russische Körper-Schutzwaffen des 9.-16. Jahrhunderts', *Zeitschrift für Historische Waffen- und Kostümkunde* (1976), 22-37.

Kirpicnikov (Kirpitchnikoff), A., 'Russische Waffen des 9.-15. Jahrhunderts', *Zeitschrift für Historische Waffen- und Kostümkunde* (1986), 1-22.

Martin, J., 'Russian Expansion in the Far North, X to mid-XVI Century', in M. Rywkin (edit.), *Russian Colonial Expansion to 1917* (London 1988), 23-43.

Meyendorff, J., *Byzantium and the Rise of Russia* (Cambridge 1981).

Michell, R., & N. Forbes (trans.), *The Chronicle of Novgorod; 1016-1471 (Camden Third Series, vol. XXV)* (London 1914).

Nicholson, H., *Templars, Hospitallers and Teutonic Knights: Images of the Military Orders, 1128-1291* (Leicester 1993).

Noonan, T.S., 'Medieval Russia, the Mongols, and the West: Novgorod's relations with the Baltic, 1100-1350', *Medieval Studies*, XXXVII (1975), 316-339.

Olins, P.Z., *The Teutonic Knights in Latvia* (Riga 1928).

Rappoport, P., 'Russian Medieval Military Architecture', *Gladius,* VIII (1969), 39-62.

Riley-Smith, J., *The Crusades: A Short History* (London 1987).

Sedov, V.V., *Finno-Ugrui i Baltui v epokhu Spednevekovya* (Finno-Ugrians and Balts in the Middle Ages) (Moscow 1987), in Russian.

Smith, J.C., & W. Urban (trans.), *The Livonian Rhymed Chronicle* (Bloomington 1977).

Thompson, M.W., *Novgorod the Great* (London 1967).

Urban, W., *The Baltic Crusade* (second revised edition, Chicago 1994).

Urban, W., 'The Organisation and Defence of the Livonian Frontier in the Thirteenth Century', *Speculum*, XLVIII (1973), 523-532.

Uustalu, E., *The History of the Estonian People* (London 1952).

Vernadsky, G., *A History of Russia, Vol. II: Kievan Russia* (New Haven 1948).

Vernadsky, G., *A History of Russia, Vol. III: The Mongols and Russia* (New Haven 1953).

Vernadsky, G., *The Origins of Russia* (Oxford 1959).

Von Der Osten-Sacken, 'Der erste Kampf des Deutschen Ordens gegen die Russen', *Mitteilungen aus dem Gebiet der Livlandischen Geschichte*, XX (1910) 87-124.

WARGAMING LAKE PEIPUS

The Battle of Lake Peipus is a tricky one to stage and did take a great deal of preparation. Firstly what rules to use? One problem is that there are a lot of good rule sets around, but they all suffer various disadvantages. The battle itself, falling in 1242 is at the end of one sub-period and the beginning of another, being neither Dark Age nor High Medieval. Then it is a clash between two different military systems; the Crusaders being west european knights, for whom virtually all medieval rules are designed, the Russians owing more to eastern europe and fitting better into Ancient rules than Medieval.

To solve this dialema I suggest that you use whatever set of rules that you personnally prefer, but be prepared to tinker with them to cope with this peculiar battle. I will describe how we went about it with *Wargame Research Groups* DBM rules, not as an unreserved recommendation, but because they are a reasonably well known set and their vocabulary can act as a lingua franca.

The other technicalities of the game such as figure and ground scale are quite easily dealt with. The game will work well with any sized figures. I decided to have a big game which allowed plenty of room for players to participate. Feel free to cut the size of the forces down to suit your circumstances. Provided everything is reduced in proportion the battle shouldn't be unbalanced because of it.

Next we have to look at the forces involved. For the Crusaders the figures are pretty reasonable, for the Russians they involve inspired guesswork. It is probable that Alexandre Nevskii's elite cavalry was approximately the same strength as their Crusader equivalent, so a thousand seems about right. Similarly it is felt that the normal estimates of the Russian force, putting it at six to seven thousand, are on the high side, are rather generous, so we cut the number back to five thousand. The best estimate for the horse archers is about 600, which leaves the infantry, whose numbers are a complete guess.

The next thing to consider is deployment. First the Crusaders. On the left are the Danes, in the centre the Bishop with his Germans, on the

The Crusaders:		Russians:	
Danish and German Knights	800	Alexanndre Nevskii's Druzhina	600
Teutonic Knights	100	Andrey Nevskii's Druzhina	400
Danes	300	Novgorod Militia	2000
Germans	400	Finno-Ugrain Tribesmen	1400
Estonian Infantry	1000	Horse arches	600

A typical piece of Estonian marshy and forested territory near Leevaku, in high summer, when such terrain formed an effective barrier against heavily armoured cavalry. In winter the same terrain was frozen hard and provided easy access for an invader. (Author's photograph)

right the Teutonic Knights, and lastly the Estonian Infantry bringing up the rear. For the Russians we have less information. After careful reading of the battle accounts we decided that the Novgorod militia infantry had to be at the front. As the Crusaders were trying to kill Alenandre Nevskii and therefore attacked headlong into the infantry in an attempt to do this he was either with the infantry, which we felt unlikely, or he was with his Druzhina behind them. This was in line with what we know of Russian tactics, wear the enemy out with the infantry before you hit them with your cavalry. As Andrey had brought the horse archers and they were on the right one can only assume that he was on that side of the battlefield. Finally the Finno-Ugrains are not mentioned in the combat so we put them at the back as a third line. This gave us a three line formation, Novogrod infantry in the front line, drawn up behind them in a second line was the cavalry, Alexandre and his Druzhina on the left, Andrey in the centre, the horse archers on the right probably not screened by infantry allowing them to more easily outflank the enemy. A third line at the back was formed by the Finno-Ugrains.

Next comes the terrain. Here I covered half my table with carpet tiles to provide a lake side. The other half represented the lake surface. Then everything was covered with a white sheet. You cannot ask for anything much easier. The problem comes when you try and decide what effect the terrain has on the battle. Now I have crossed a frozen shallow lake on foot, during the thaw. This was in Iceland rather that in Russia but I suspect that conditions are similar. Here I found that the lake was covered with very thin ice on top of melt water from the surrounding land which itself was on top of the main icesheet left over from winter. Under this was the water from the lake and below this was the lake bed, frozen solid and an excellent surface to walk on. I would suggest that at the edge the horses broke through the ice but got a firm footing on the ice bed and advanced on that. They would have lost momentum but would not have been thrown into disorder. Hence we gave anyone at the top of the bank an advantage over anyone at the bottom of the bank, in the lake. In DBM terms this meant that the infantry got a +1 for being uphill, this was I felt all the situation deserved.

The next thing that we have to consider is the actual troop types who fought at the battle. First the Crusaders. The infantry should be of the poorest quality, 'Horde' in DBM terms. The cavalry were all knights but here the complications start creeping in. The Teutonic knights should be better than the average, so in DBM 'Inferior' knights. The term is a bit misleading but the effect achieved under the rules is what you are looking for. Finally Danish knights were old fashioned and a bit backward, so if possible have them more lightly armoured, DBM 'Fast' knights fitted the bill. I realise that I've added rather a lot of chrome here, you can just treat them all as standard knights and still have a balanced battle.

The Russian cavalry are also easy to categorise. The Druzhnas are standard cavalry. They might have been a social elite but in strictly military terms they were just decent irregular cavalry. The Bases representing the two Nevskii brothers we did allow to be superior. The horse archers are whatever our rules categorise competent light cavalry horse archers as.

The Russian infantry are difficult. Here DBM has problems. Covering the whole ancient and medieval period good infantry was the exception rather than the rule and the Novgorod militia, good enough in their day, don't stand close comparison with Greek mercenary Hoplites or Roman Legionaires. Reading the battle account it is clear that the knights got in amongst the infantry and the cavalry coming in from the flanks were necessary to win the battle. Look through any wargames rule set and you will find that decent infantry up hill of knights, need no rescuing. Here a period specific rule set will win out in that it should allow for infantry bad enough to be troubled by mounted troops, even with the advantage of position. We got around the problem by classing the Novgorod militia as 'Horde'. This also gave us a classification for the Finno-Ugrains. Had they been better than the Novogrod militia they would have been more prominent. The cynic might also say that had they been better than the militia, they wouldn't have been part of the Novogrod sphere of influence in the first place.

As I said I'm using DBM terms as a lingua franca. Also feel free to increase or decrease the size of the forces providing you keep the proportions the same.

Having laid out your forces on the table the next thing to do is to organise them. I suggest each of the contingents mentioned in the list is treated as a separate regiment, unit, command. I would also suggest that for morale purposes no-one takes any notice of a unit composed entirely of horde routs. In this game the lower orders know their place.

Now then we have to look at various options which can be added to the game. I suppose it could be argued that if the Russians wipe the Crusader force out they can call it a draw, but in all other circumstances, without Alexandre they are effectively beaten. To stop the Russians hiding him at the back out of harms way I reccommend another rule. If Alexandre's Druzhna is in combat and Alexandre is not fighting or des-

Suggested figures to use:

The Crusaders
Teutonic Knights. 2 bases Reg Kn (S)
Danes. 6 bases Irreg Kn (F)
Germans. 8 DBM bases. Keg Kn (I)
Estonian Infantry. 20 bases Horde.

Russians
Alexandre Nevskii's Druzhina. 12 bases Irreg Cv (O)
Andrey Nevskii's Druzhina. 8 bases Irreg Cv (O)
Novgorod Miitia. 40 bases Horde
Finno-Ugrain Tribesmen. 28 bases Horde.

A German bronze aquamanile or decorative 'jug' of the 13th century in the form of a knight with a spear, a flat-topped great helm and perhaps originally a shield. (Museo Civico Medievale, Bologna)

perately trying to get into the melee, the Druzhina counts as demoralised/each figure gets-1.

The second thing to look at is the frozen lake. When charging from the lake onto the bank you have the lake bed acting as a ramp, going the other way you are confronted by the problem of getting up onto the ice surface while in the water. Effectively the ice edge can act as a one way ditch. Once the Knights had climbed onto the bank I marked out an area behind them which they could get stuck in, needing a roll of 4, 5, 6 on a d6 per base to get back on to the ice to escape.

The third Crusader problem is the Estonian Infantry. Just how bad were they? Looking at the original battle they might have attempted to follow the cavalry and found that the breaking of the ice had left them with a moat to cross. Remember a mounted knight could cross this obstacle provided his horses head stayed above water. For an infantryman that depth of icy water was a death trap. If you crossed it you would almost certainly die of exposure, even without the gentle ministrations of the Novgorod militia. Alternatively the Estonians may merely have been unenthusiastic and on being given half a chance, ran off. I would give them the following options. Firstly you could assume a degree of enthusiasm, but don't allow them to follow in the tracks of the knights. The other option is to say that should they suffer any casualties they break and run, never to return. Indeed in post battle discussion the Crusader commander felt that just having the umpire arbitrarily pointing to the Estonians and announcing their rout for no obvious reason would be a suitable alternative.

The Russians have less reasonable alternatives that you can try. However be warned, virtually anything that you do improves their already good chances of winning. One option is to assume that the Novgorod militia were reasonable infantry. They should be a 50/50 mixture of irregular spearmen and archers. The problem with this option and deployment is that the game lacks zest for the Crusader player. Being contemptuously butchered in the water by competent infantry isn't the most enjoyable way to spend an evening.

Another Russian option is to change the deployment. Changing the Crusader set up isn't really viable as you no longer get the battle of Lake Peipus, indeed the game is very suitable for Russian solo play. For the Russians one alternative formation is with the cavalry centre looking for Alexandre while the Teutonic knights rampage through the flanking infantry. In this option I would make the Novgorod infantry a mix of spearmen and archers, the arrow storm from the flanks combined with the slope should allow the Russian cavalry some hope of success without loading everything too much in their favour.

No matter which option you choose I would recommend that you give this battle a try, it is a lot closer and more interesting than you would think.

Side view of a late 13th century carved capital showing
Teutonic Knights jousting. It came from the castle of
the Chapter of Pomezania at Kwidzin. The armour is
old fashioned and differed only slightly from that used
at the battle of Lake Peipus.
(inv. MZM/ DA/ 5, Malbork Castle Museum, Poland)